Reading
Shakespeare
Today

A MIDSUMMER NIGHT'S DREAM

Patricia Wagner and Summar West

Cavendish
Square

New York

Published in 2017 by Cavendish Square Publishing, LLC
243 5th Avenue, Suite 136, New York, NY 10016

Copyright © 2017 by Cavendish Square Publishing, LLC

First Edition

Website: cavendishsq.com

Library of Congress Cataloging-in-Publication Data

Names: Wagner, Patricia, author | West, Summar, author.
Title: A midsummer night's dream / Patricia Wagner and Summar West.
Description: New York: Cavendish Square, 2017. |
Series: Reading Shakespeare today | Includes index.
Identifiers: ISBN 9781502623355 (library bound) | ISBN 9781502623362 (ebook)
Subjects: LCSH: Shakespeare, William, 1564-1616.
Midsummer night's dream--Juvenile literature.
Classification: LCC PR2827.W28 2017 | DDC 822.3'3--dc23

Editorial Director: David McNamara
Editor: Caitlyn Miller
Copy Editor: Rebecca Rohan
Associate Art Director: Amy Greenan
Designer: Lindsey Auten
Production Coordinator: Karol Szymczuk
Photo Research: J8 Media

The photographs in this book are used by permission and through the courtesy of: Shutterstock.com, front, back cove
and background throughout the book; Photo credits: Cover Angela Weiss/Getty Images for The Broad Stage; p. 7 Priva
Collection/Bridgeman Images; p. 10 DEA/G. DAGLI ORTI/Getty Images; p. 14 Bettmann/Getty Images; p. 15 Albert Mold
National Geographic/Getty Images; p. 16-17 Wenceslaus Hollar/File:1647 Long view of London From Bankside -Wences
Hollar.jpg/Wikimedia Commons; p. 18 Kamira/Shutterstock.com; p. 23 Bettmann/Getty Images; p. 25 © Niday Picture Lib
Alamy Stock Photo; p. 27 © Summerfield Press/CORBIS/Corbis via Getty Images; p. 29 Bettmann/Getty Images; p. 3
CALLE TOERNSTROEM/REUTERS/Newscom; p. 33 TOUCHSTONE PICTURES/Album/Album; p. 35 20th Century-F
Getty Images; p. 36 United Archives GmbH/Alamy Stock Photo; p. 38 David Farrell/Getty Images; p. 40 Joseph Noel Pat
File:Sir Joseph Noel Paton - The Quarrel of Oberon and Titania - Google Art Project 2.jpg/Wikimedia Commons, ; p. 42 E
Henry Landseer/File:Edwin Landseer - Scene from A Midsummer Night's Dream. Titania; p. and Bottom - Google Art Pro
jpg/Wikimedia Commons; p. 47 Angela Weiss/Getty Images for The Broad Stage; p. 49 Tunbridge/Tunbridge-Sedgwic
Pictorial Press/Getty Images; p. 51 © Christie's Images/Bridgeman Images; p. 64 JB Vincent/Shutterstock.com, ; p. 71 W
Shakespeare, Richard Bradock and Thomas Fisher/File:First Quarto Printing of A Midsummer Night's Dream.jpg/Wikime
Commons; p. 75 William Shakespeare, Valentine Simmes (printer), Andrew Wise (publisher), William Aspley/File:First Qu
of Much Ado About Nothing.jpg/Wikimedia Commons; p. 76 Tom Herde/The Boston Globe via Getty Images; p. 79 © Ge
Lewis/Alamy Stock Photo; p. 84 © Geraint Lewis/Alamy Stock Photo; p. 88 Jonathan Blair/Corbis via Getty Images.

Printed in the United States of America

CONTENTS

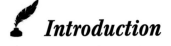

SHAKESPEARE AND HIS WORLD

While some may call him a genius and others may argue he is the greatest writer in English literature, what we can say with certainty is that William Shakespeare is a writer whose work has been immortalized. Though centuries have passed since Shakespeare first penned his plays, they continue to be read and adapted for movies, television, ballet, opera, radio, comic books, and more. As the nineteenth-century poet Ben Jonson wrote of Shakespeare, his work was not limited to one time period only, "but for all time."

Most scholars agree that Shakespeare was born in Stratford-upon-Avon in England in 1564 and was baptized on April 26th of that year. His father, John Shakespeare, was a glove maker and town officer who often struggled financially. While there is speculation that William could have attended a local grammar school due to his father's job, it is uncertain how or if he received a formal education; this and many other biographical details remain unknown due to a lack of primary sources.

Another important date is the year that Shakespeare married; in 1582, at the age of eighteen, he married Anne Hathaway, who was eight years older. Their daughter Susanna was born six months later, and the next year their twins, Hamnet and Judith, were born. A parish burial register indicates that tragedy struck the family years later when Shakespeare's son Hamnet died at the age of eleven.

According to records from the 1590s, Shakespeare's career began as a member of the Lord Chamberlain's Men, a leading acting company in London. His work as a writer garnered him attention with the publication of his poems *Venus and Adonis* in 1593 and *The Rape of Lucrece* in 1594. Both poems were very successful and launched his reputation as a major poet. Today, we remember his poetry best by the 154 sonnets that he wrote.

While Shakespeare is still lauded as a great poet, we continue to regard many of his plays as some of the greatest works of literature ever written. By 1594, Shakespeare's plays began to appear in print, and by 1598, they bore his name. In the beginning of his playwriting career, he was associated with plays about English history and comedies, but his tragedies are considered by many to be his greatest achievement. Some of his most widely read tragedies include *Julius Caesar, Hamlet, Romeo and Juliet*, and *Macbeth*. Comedies that continue to delight audiences include *A Midsummer Night's Dream, Much Ado About Nothing*, and *As You Like It*.

Four hundred years after his death in 1616, Shakespeare's presence remains. The body of his work was preserved for us through the First Folio, a collection of his writing produced by his King's Men colleagues in 1623. The First Folio was published under the title *The Comedies, Histories, and Tragedies of Mr. William Shakespeare*. Today, hundreds of years later, William Shakespeare lives on through performances of his plays, creative adaptations of his works, and his monumental influence on the English language.

 *Chapter One*

Shakespeare and *A Midsummer Night's Dream*

A Midsummer Night's Dream, one of Shakespeare's first masterpieces, has always been one of his most popular plays. Certainly it is the silliest, with confusing pairs of quarreling lovers, mischievous fairies, ignorant rustics, and, of course, a comical donkey's head.

Among his best plays, *A Midsummer Night's Dream* is Shakespeare's purest comedy, furthest from tragedy, except for a brief moment in the opening scene. The play also has some of his simplest and most enchanting poetry, as evidenced in this scene that relays part of the dreamlike world of the fairies that is described by Oberon, their king:

> *I know a bank where the wild thyme blows,*
> *Where oxlips and the nodding violet grows,*

This painting by Frank Cadogan Cowper shows Titania sleeping in a lush forest.

Quite overcanopied with luscious woodbine
With sweet musk-roses, and with eglantine.
There sleeps Titania sometime of the night,
Lulled in these flowers with dances and delight.

Oberon's soliloquy is one among many in the play where audiences hear a very different dramatic language than that used in some of Shakespeare's previous plays like *Richard III* and *The Taming of the Shrew*.

Many scholars suspect that Shakespeare wrote *A Midsummer Night's Dream* for an important wedding around 1595; in fact, some scholars believe that it was written for an aristocratic wedding that Queen Elizabeth attended. The play was first printed in 1600, was reprinted in 1619, and again in the First Folio of the collected plays in

1623. As the title implies, the whole play has the quality of a happy dream, in which there is no evil or serious danger to anyone, and everything ends happily for all concerned. Most of the action occurs in a single night, and all is resolved in the end.

As a rule, Shakespeare borrowed his plots from known sources, usually published before 1603. Some sources were very ancient, whether historical or mythological. *A Midsummer Night's Dream* is an exception. He seems to have invented the whole story himself, though some scholars argue that there is evidence to suggest that the playwright was drawing upon memorable scenes from his own childhood and from the folklore of his culture that would've been familiar to him. Whatever the sources, the play includes five plot points that are woven together: the wedding of Theseus and Hippolyta; the struggle between the king and queen of the fairies, Oberon and Titania; the various relationships between the four young, human couples; the mishaps and adventures of Bottom; and the play put on by the tradesmen.

The setting and some of the chief characters of the play are nominally ancient Greek, but the fairies and homely tradesmen smack of Shakespeare's English countryside. He appears to have a special affection for this material and for the circle of friends of the simple Bottom, his greatest buffoon and one of his most endearing creations.

The play uses more rhyme than any of his other plays, lending it a unique air of enchantment. Many scholars suspect that Titania, queen of the fairies, is a playful tribute to Queen Elizabeth I herself, who was saluted in Edmund Spenser's great poem *The Faerie Queene*. Regardless of whether or not the play was a tribute to the queen, in the England of Queen Elizabeth I, plays were enjoyed by all classes of people, though they were not yet respected as a serious form of art. The spectators probably reacted rowdily to the play, not listening in reverent silence. After all, they had come to have fun! Furthermore, audience members were largely uneducated. This presented playwrights with a unique challenge: a play had to amuse people who could not read.

We must bear in mind that when the play was performed in the London theater, it had to be shortened and perhaps simplified somewhat; Shakespeare's theater had almost no special effects. Plays may have been extremely popular, but they were also primitive. They were performed outdoors in the afternoon, since there were no electric lights. (Therefore, Shakespeare's lines that remind us of when the action is occurring—whether by day or at night, by the light of the moon and stars—are necessary.) Often the "theater" was only an enclosed courtyard. Probably the versions of Shakespeare's plays that we know today were not used in full, but shortened to about two hours for actual performance. Poorer spectators (illiterate "groundlings") stood on the ground around it, at times exposed to rain and snow. Wealthier people sat in raised tiers above. Aside from some costumes, there were few props or special effects and almost no scenery. Much had to be imagined: whole battles might be represented by a few actors with swords. Thunder might be simulated by rattling a sheet of tin offstage.

The plays were far from realistic and, under the conditions of the time, could hardly try to be. Above the rear of the main stage was a small balcony. (It was this balcony from which Juliet spoke to Romeo.) Ghosts and

Queen Elizabeth I might have served as Shakespeare's inspiration for the character Titania; plays were immensely popular during her reign.

witches might appear by entering through a trapdoor in the stage floor. Unlike the modern theater, Shakespeare's Globe Theatre—he describes it as "this wooden O"—had no curtain separating the stage from the audience. This allowed intimacy between the players and the spectators.

Since the audience had to engage more actively in listening to the play, Shakespeare could only use part of the full text; the lines were also written to be spoken loudly. In many ways, his plays are now easier to perform on film than on the stage, but in film, where the microphone picks up even the lowest sounds, the lines may be spoken in a normal tone of voice, or even whispered.

The Evolution of the Theater

In order to understand *A Midsummer Night's Dream*, as well as Shakespeare's other plays, it is a good idea to know more about their theatrical background. During the reign of Queen Elizabeth I, from 1558 to 1603, the theater became extremely popular, not only in London, but throughout England. Plays had long been performed in courtyards and by law students at the Inns of Court, a collection of buildings where they lived and studied. By the 1580s, however, regular theaters were built to accommodate large crowds of spectators. Actors such as Edward Alleyn, Richard Burbage (later a partner in Shakespeare's company, the King's Men), and the clown Will Kempe became huge stars.

Plays were also acted at the queen's court and even in large private homes. Some rich lords, such as the Earl of Oxford, employed their own companies of actors in their households to entertain guests, especially on special occasions. The comical production of *Pyramus and Thisby*

Shakespeare in the Parks

WHILE THERE ARE vast differences between the world of Shakespeare's plays and ours, one tradition that has continued is that of outdoor theater. Theater companies around the world create outdoor productions that are often free to the public. These productions sometimes coincide with festivals and workshops and take place during the summer.

In New York City, the Public Theater has hosted Free Shakespeare in the Park at the Delacorte Theater for nearly sixty years. During the summer, you can bring your own food and drinks for the show at this free outdoor theater, where Hollywood stars such as Meryl Streep, Al Pacino, and Anne Hathaway have been known to grace the stage.

The Public Theater also sponsors an exciting initiative called the Public Works, where members of the community are invited to participate in classes, workshops, and performances with the goal of creating participatory theater. Who knows what Shakespeare would have thought of this blurring between professional and amateur actors, but Public Works is certainly fostering a love of Shakespeare and building community.

In Shakespeare's own hometown of Stratford-upon-Avon, the Royal Shakespeare Company invites groups to apply to perform at its outdoor theater, the Dell, during the summer. The theater has now hosted more than 250 groups inspired by the Bard. Another popular outdoor festival in England is the Cambridge Shakespeare Festival that runs for eight weeks every summer.

Bard on the Beach, 2010

For those who want to experience a summer of Shakespeare by the sea, there's the Bard on the Beach Shakespeare Festival in Vancouver. The festival provides affordable productions of plays, educational workshops, as well as community gathering spaces in the Bard Village, all of which is located along the beautiful waterfront of Vancouver's Vanier Park.

These are but a few of the many experiences that can be found when searching for Shakespearean summer activities!

The Globe Theatre as it was during Shakespeare's lifetime

at Theseus's wedding in *A Midsummer Night's Dream* may reflect this custom. Plays were performed in London, of course, at the Universities of Oxford and Cambridge, and even in towns around the country by touring companies.

It is also important to keep in mind some of the more difficult and dire parts of the context of Elizabethan England. Transportation was not only difficult but slow, chiefly by horse and boat. Most people were illiterate peasants who lived on farms that they seldom left; cities grew up along waterways and were subject to frequent plagues that could wipe out much of the population within weeks. Money—in coin form, not paper—was scarce and hardly existed outside the cities. By today's standards, even the rich were poor. Life was precarious. Most children died young, and famine or disease might kill anyone at any time. Everyone was familiar with death. Starvation was not rare or remote, as it is to most of us

This modern-day staging of a Shakespeare play shows just how far theaters have come in the past four hundred years!

today. Medical care was poor and might kill as many people as it healed.

During that period, England was also torn by religious conflict, often violent, among Roman Catholics who were loyal to the Pope, adherents of the Church of England who were loyal to the queen, and the Puritans who would take over the country in the revolution of 1642. This was the grim background of Shakespeare's theater during the reign of Queen Elizabeth I, but this man from Stratford-upon-Avon pursued his work.

Until the 1590s, there were almost no records of plays' performances, but by 1589 a version of *Hamlet* (most scholars doubt that it was Shakespeare's version) was being performed in one of the public theaters, along with huge successes such as *The Spanish Tragedy* (thought to be written by Thomas Kyd). In 1598, Francis Meres published a list of Shakespeare's tragedies and comedies,

The politics of 1600s England affected the transmission of Shakespeare's work.

naming six of each, and *A Midsummer Night's Dream* was listed as one of the comedies.

In 1599, Shakespeare's company, the Lord Chamberlain's Men (later known as the King's Men), built the Globe Theatre, and many of Shakespeare's greatest plays were first performed there. (A modern replica of the Globe was built on the original site in London; it specializes, naturally, in Shakespeare.) Other leading acting companies included Lord Strange's Men and Lord Sussex's Men.

After Elizabeth I died in 1603, the new king, James I (who was also James VI of Scotland), became the patron of the Lord Chamberlain's Men, who were then renamed the King's Men. *A Midsummer Night's Dream* was performed at James's court under the title *A Play of Robin Goodfellow* on New Year's night in 1604. Today, King James is best remembered for another literary achievement: he sponsored the greatest English translation of the Bible, the Authorized Version. Still popularly known as the King James Version, it was published in 1611. Only Shakespeare's works have had a comparable impact on the English language.

During this time, the popularity of the theater continued to grow, and by 1610, indoor theaters began to arise. In 1613, a fire destroyed the Globe during a

performance of *Henry VIII*, one of Shakespeare's last plays. Despite this, plays went on flourishing until 1642, the year the Puritan Revolution overthrew King Charles I (he was beheaded in 1649) and outlawed the theaters, which the Puritans had always hated. *A Midsummer Night's Dream* kept its popularity even during the years of Puritan rule, when it was performed illegally and secretly at fairs and taverns around the English countryside.

The theaters remained closed until 1660, when the Puritans themselves were overthrown and Charles's son, Charles II, was restored to the throne. But by then Shakespeare's company was gone; the old theaters and their traditions were gone, too. The theater had to start over. A new era, which was called the Restoration theater, revived Shakespeare's plays, often drastically adapting them to suit new tastes. Now plays were performed indoors at night, illuminated by candlelight. Women could legally appear upon the stage for the first time, and morals were more relaxed. Despite the fact that the Puritans were out of power, they remained influential.

During this time, Shakespeare's reputation declined. He was still popular, but many people, influenced by French fashions, regarded him as crude and somewhat barbarous. Samuel Pepys saw a production of *A Midsummer Night's Dream* in 1662 and wrote in his diary that it was

The restored Globe Theatre

"the most insipid ridiculous play that ever I saw in my life." Nahum Tate, England's poet laureate, actually rewrote some of Shakespeare's plays completely, giving his darkest tragedy, *King Lear*, a happy ending! Tate's version was performed on the stage for more than a century, during which Shakespeare's original remained almost unknown.

Other plays by the Bard suffered the same fate. The poets John Dryden and William Davenant (who claimed to be Shakespeare's son!) were among the many people who tried to "improve" the plays but chiefly succeeded only in mutilating them. Today, these supposed "improvements" are rarely performed and have been almost totally forgotten. Instead, Shakespeare's work has found its way into modern culture in a myriad of forms.

Not only are Shakespeare's plays performed and adapted in other mediums, but they are staged by cultures around the world; furthermore, some scholars argue that many of the ideas that societies think of as their own were originally scripted by Shakespeare and that he is woven into both high and low culture. In her book, *Shakespeare and Modern Culture*, scholar Marjorie Garber makes this very argument: that as much as modern culture shapes Shakespeare, the world's greatest playwright continues to shape modern culture.

 *Chapter Two*

The Play's the Thing

While much of the action of *A Midsummer Night's Dream* takes place in a more enchanted world, it begins in the human world. And of course in order for the play—even one that is a comedy rather than a drama—to develop its characters and themes, we need conflict; that conflict for the human characters (and later for others) occurs rather quickly in this particular play.

Act I, Scene 1

Overview

The story of *A Midsummer Night's Dream* begins with interrupted festivity. Theseus, the duke of Athens, is about to marry Hippolyta, the queen of the Amazons (female warriors), whom he has just defeated in battle. But his loving murmurs to his bride-to-be—the wedding is only four days off—are cut short by the sudden arrival of the angry Egeus, an Athenian nobleman.

Egeus is furious because his daughter Hermia refuses to marry Demetrius, the man he has chosen for her; instead she wants to marry her lover, Lysander. Egeus demands that she be put to death if she disobeys him. He petitions Theseus because, as duke, Theseus represents power and is an upholder of Athenian law.

The gentle Theseus knows that the cruel law is on Egeus's side, and he warns Hermia that unless she marries Demetrius, she must either "die the death" or live the rest of her life as a nun, seeing no men, having no children, and "chanting faint hymns to the cold fruitless moon." He gives her only until his own wedding day to decide whether to marry Demetrius or to "prepare to die" for "disobedience to your father's will."

Now Lysander boldly steps forward to assert his own right to marry Hermia. Never mind the law, he tells Theseus; he loves Hermia more than Demetrius does, and she loves him, too. According to Lysander, Demetrius is also "inconstant"; he has wooed another young woman, Helena, caused her to fall madly in love with him, and then jilted her.

Theseus admits that Lysander has a point. He, too, has heard about Demetrius's dishonorable treatment of Helena, but, being busy with his own wedding plans, he has had no time to inquire further. Still, the law is the law. Once again, he tells Hermia that she must submit to "your father's will" or choose between "death" and (softening the penalty somewhat) "a vow of single life."

"Come, my Hippolyta: what cheer, my love?" says Theseus as the case is disposed of. This line deftly suggests that Hippolyta's sympathies are with the lovers, not with the harsh law of Athens.

As the others leave to prepare for the great wedding, Hermia and Lysander remain alone together. As she weeps, he comments: "The course of true love never did run smooth." Even without external obstacles and enemies, he notes, love is often "short as any dream."

But he has a happy idea: they can run away together! He proposes that they meet in the forest outside Athens the next night. From there they can go for help to his aunt, a rich widow who lives a few miles away, beyond the reach of "the sharp Athenian law." "There, gentle Hermia," Lysander says, "may I marry thee." She joyfully agrees.

Just then Helena, Hermia's old friend and "playfellow," arrives. Helena pours out her heart, begging Hermia to tell her how she won Demetrius's love, which she wants so badly. Hermia cannot understand it herself: "I give him curses, yet he gives me love." Helena has the opposite problem: "The more I love, the more he hateth me."

Lysander and Hermia tell Helena about their plan to elope, then they leave her alone. After reflecting on the nature of love, she decides to betray her friend and reveal the elopement plan to Demetrius, hoping he will thank her as he pursues Hermia in the woods.

Analysis

Egeus may seem extreme to us in demanding his daughter's death, but under ancient Greek and Roman law, a father, as head of the family (or *paterfamilias*), had the legal authority to put any member of his family to death. Usually this was done only to unwanted infants, but disobedient children and unfaithful wives might also at times be subject to this ultimate penalty. Jews and Christians were, of course, shocked by this harsh pagan law, and after the ancient world converted to Christianity, it was abolished.

Hermia and Lysander

Writing for his Christian audience in England, Shakespeare wants us to be a little shocked, too. Will Hermia have to die? This happiest of comedies begins with that grim question. But, of course, we really know she will not die; the question is how she will escape the law. Our slight anxiety for her life is just enough to involve our sympathy and start the action of the play moving.

The four lovers are hard to tell apart. Hermia? Helena? Which is which? The close similarity of their names is a clue that Shakespeare is playing with our memories, trying to confuse us a little. Given his matchless genius for creating vivid characters, the effect here must be deliberate: four major characters are made indistinct—like figures in a dream.

Helena, when alone, speaks directly to the audience in a soliloquy. In plays, soliloquies can involve a single character speaking either to the audience or to herself, though soliloquies can also be a representation of the character's inner thoughts. Shakespeare often uses the soliloquy to give the audience information, to let a character express his or her innermost thoughts, or to introduce important themes of the play. On film, the character may speak the soliloquy aloud (just as on the stage), or the actor may be silent, seen in close-up, while the speech is heard as a voice-over.

In this rhyming speech, Helena speaks less for herself than for the whole play:

Things base and vile, holding no quantity,
Love can transpose to form and dignity.
Love looks not with the eyes, but with the mind,
And therefore is wing'd Cupid painted blind.

Shakespeare intentionally gave Hermia and Helena similar names to give audiences a taste of the confusion his characters would soon face.

Just what does all this mean? It is somewhat mysterious; while we may accept the mystery and the flow of the poetry, we have a sense that appearance alone isn't all that matters when it comes to love. However, we do know that the reference to Cupid in the soliloquy refers to the son of Venus, goddess of love. He caused people to fall in love by shooting arrows into their hearts. Artists often represented him in pictures as either blind or blindfolded, implying that love is irrational. This also speaks to a certain lack of control when it comes to love.

Throughout *A Midsummer Night's Dream*, Shakespeare reminds us of the problematic nature of love. Does it begin in the eyes or the mind? Is it above reason or below it? Wise or fickle? There is no single answer to all these questions, except that love is basic and irresistible, the joy and essence of life.

Helena speaks of "eyes" several times in this speech. This is a chief motif of the play, which contains dozens of mentions of eyes (or *eyne*, the old plural form), sight, blindness, light, darkness, day, night, sleep, waking (or "half sleep, half waking"), and, of course, dreaming—lots of dreaming. We are seldom fully sure of what is real and what is unreal.

Act I, Scene 2

Overview

A group of tradesmen, the mechanicals, gather to rehearse a play, or "interlude," to be performed at the wedding of Theseus and Hippolyta. The play is "the most lamentable comedy, and most cruel death, of Pyramus and Thisby." Actually, the old story of Pyramus and

Cupid can be seen at the top of this famous painting by Botticelli.

Thisby has a tragic plot, the source of Shakespeare's own *Romeo and Juliet* (which itself is often viewed as the tragic "twin" of *A Midsummer Night's Dream* for its sweet, youthful, and frequently comic flavor). Pyramus and Thisby's warring families forbid them to marry, and they ultimately kill themselves.

The unschooled amateur actors get everything wrong. Peter Quince, the carpenter, is their leader, but Nick Bottom, the weaver, insists on stealing the show. First, he wants to star as Pyramus; he promises to make the audience weep. But when Francis Flute, the bellows-mender, begs off on the role of "Thisby" because "I have a beard coming," Bottom offers to play that part, too. Then he decides he wants to play the roaring lion: "I will make the duke say, 'Let him roar again, let him roar again.'"

Analysis

In this scene, written in homely prose befitting the low characters, Shakespeare's mechanicals begin to take over the play, especially the sublimely funny Nick Bottom, one of Shakespeare's greatest characters. At this point, we see only Bottom's ridiculous conceit; he is funny enough, but there is no hint of the comic destiny that lies ahead for him later in the story, when the natural and the supernatural will meet and interact. Shakespeare is carefully preparing us for a delirious and unpredictable comic climax.

Just as Shakespeare loves to blend opposites, such as comedy and tragedy, here he sees to it that these bumbling actors will turn the tragedy of Pyramus and Thisby into a "lamentable comedy."

Act II, Scene 1

Overview

Oberon, king of the fairies, is estranged from his wife, Titania. They are quarreling over a little boy, a changeling "stolen from an Indian king." We learn from Puck, Oberon's chief lieutenant, that Oberon wants the boy but Titania refuses to give him up. After Puck has explained this to another fairy, Oberon and Titania themselves appear, he demanding the child, she still refusing. They trade accusations; she says he loves Hippolyta, and he retorts that she loves Theseus. When Titania departs, Oberon summons Puck and orders him to fetch a magic flower whose juice causes sleepers to fall in love with the first live creature they see when they awaken. He will use this to take his revenge on his wife. As Puck

William Blake's illustration of the play's fairies, including Oberon, Titania, and Puck

departs, Oberon makes himself invisible and watches as poor Helena pursues the scornful Demetrius, who orders her to leave. When they are gone, Puck returns with the charmed flower. Oberon, pitying Helena, now directs Puck to drop its juice into the eyes of a sleeping Athenian youth. Puck promises to obey, but now the confusion begins! Oberon has neglected to tell him which person is Demetrius, the intended recipient of the juice.

Analysis

In this scene, written in some of Shakespeare's most bewitching poetry, we enter the supernatural world of the fairies. And we find that they, like the mortals they try to dominate with their magical powers, are far from infallible. In fact they are petty, jealous, and foolish—much too sure of themselves. Greater power does not confer greater wisdom. To paraphrase Puck's most famous line: Lord, what fools these fairies be! (The wisest character in the play will turn out to be a human: Theseus.) We are touched when Demetrius cruelly insults poor, sweet Helena as she pours out her love for him. Someone is about to get his comeuppance.

Act II, Scene 2

Overview

Titania enters with her fairies, and she orders them to sing her to sleep. As she dozes, Oberon sneaks by and squeezes the juice of the flower onto her eyelids. As he departs, Lysander and Hermia arrive. Weary after their flight from Athens, they fall asleep—and Puck finds them. Mistaking Lysander for the Athenian youth whom Oberon had spoken of, he applies the magic flower's juice and exits, not realizing what he has done.

Now Demetrius arrives, still pursued by Helena. As he leaves her alone, Helena sees Lysander and wakes him. He immediately falls in love with her, tells her so, and adds that his "reason," now mature, has made him fall out of love with Hermia, for "reason says you are the worthier maid." Helena doesn't believe him; she naturally assumes that he is making cruel fun of her. She leaves, and Lysander says he is now sick of Hermia and hates her. She awakens just as he has departed, crying out to him to protect her from a serpent she has been dreaming of. But she finds he has gone.

Analysis

Now this silly play—or is the whole thing just a dream?—goes into high gear. Everyone is confused; none of the

The confusion and ridiculousness of the play lend themselves to humorous stagings.

characters comprehend what is going on. They have no individuality; one seems to turn into the other and back again. Shakespeare has fun keeping the audience as mixed up as the lovers. And Lysander thinks it is his "reason" that controls his heart! But worse is yet to come. We have barely met Nick Bottom.

Act III, Scene 1

Overview

As Titania, invisible to them, lies asleep nearby, the "actors" gather in the woods to rehearse the play that they plan to put on for the wedding of Theseus and Hippolyta. As usual, Nick Bottom insists on dominating the whole production. First, he objects that when Pyramus stabs himself to death, the ladies in the audience will be terrified. Therefore, he says, a prologue must be spoken to assure everyone that Pyramus is only an actor and that his suicide is not real.

Bottom raises the further objection that the lion, "a fearful wild-fowl," will also frighten the ladies. Should a second prologue be added to tell them that the beast, too, is only an actor? Again, Bottom has the answer: the actor himself must be named, his face must be seen through the lion's neck, and he must address the ladies to tell them that he is not actually a lion, saying: "No, I am no such thing, I am a man as other men are."

As further problems arise, it is agreed that two other actors must impersonate the moon, by whose light Pyramus and Thisby see each other, and the wall through which they speak to each other.

Just then Puck, who is invisible on this occasion, arrives to eavesdrop. When Bottom steps away from the group to await his cue, Puck changes Bottom's head to a donkey's head without Bottom knowing it. Seeing the transformed Bottom, the other actors flee in terror, and Bottom, not understanding, thinks they are trying to scare *him.*

Left alone, Bottom sings. This awakens Titania, who, under the magic flower's spell, thinks she is hearing an angelic voice. Seeing Bottom, she tells him that she adores his lovely voice as well as his beauty, begs him to sing again, and swears her love for him. When he replies with a joke, she coos, in all seriousness: "Thou art as wise as thou art beautiful." She summons her attendant fairies, Peaseblossom, Cobweb, Moth, and Mustardseed, to bring him fruits and honey and make him comfortable in every way. Bottom makes their acquaintance with comical courtesy, noticing nothing out of the ordinary.

Analysis

This scene reaches one of Shakespeare's comic pinnacles. No reader or spectator can ever forget the play's immortal emblematic image of Bottom with an ass's head. It is as indelible as Hamlet holding poor Yorick's skull, Juliet speaking to Romeo from her balcony, or Macbeth facing the three Weird Sisters—fixed in our mind's eye forever.

The scene opens with the actors fretting absurdly about their play's going wrong if the audience fails to distinguish fiction from reality. A riot of misunderstanding ensues. When Titania professes her love to Bottom, he replies, "Methinks, mistress, you should have little reason for that. And yet, to say the truth, reason and love keep little company together nowadays." This is a shrewd comment on the whole play, and the fact that it

A still image from Julie Taymor's *Tempest* shows how Shakespeare's plays have become high-tech films.

Shakespeare's Shifts in the Digital Age

MUCH HAS CHANGED since the Elizabethan productions of Shakespeare's plays, when sunlight provided light, actors were responsible for their own makeup and could only wear costumes according to their social rank, and every play featured an all-male cast. Special effects on stage and in films now go well beyond fireworks, live animals, and trapdoors; certainly female actors are abundantly present in plays, costume design and makeup are elaborate art forms, and even the genders of characters are swapped at times in modern stagings. A small sampling of some of these shifts gives insight into just how much the plays have transformed.

A Midsummer Night's Dream is one of the most common plays to see staged during the summer, but the contemporary staging of this play is anything but ordinary. The *New York Times* ran an article in June of 2013 giving an overview of a wide variety of different performances staged, including a version of the play set in the 1960s, a 1920s Jazz Age production, and a Victorian-era setting. An online version of the play borne from a collaboration between the Royal Shakespeare Company and the Google Creative Lab was perhaps the most unusual adaptation mentioned.

Yet it seems that technology's prevalent role in adapting Shakespeare's plays is here to stay. We see tech's influence in films particularly, whether it's director Baz Luhrmann's *Romeo and Juliet*—which begins with a televised news report that opens the tale of the star-crossed lovers—or director Julie Taymor's version

Baz Lurhmann's *Romeo and Juliet*

of *The Tempest*, where computer-generated special effects for the character of Ariel look like something out of a music video.

Perhaps Shakespeare would be impressed by the ways that his plots, characters, and settings can be enhanced on stage or screen, and perhaps he would be surprised by the cultural move from male-centered plays to adaptations like Taymor's where the lead character of Prospero has changed genders to become Prospera. We can only wonder what Shakespeare would make of the myriad interpretations of his work.

Puck and Oberon are about to complicate matters further.

comes incongruously from its greatest dolt is part of the fun of this comedy: Shakespeare keeps playing with the theme of love's irrationality, so, in a way, we feel that it is fitting when his most foolish character speaks one of the story's deepest truths.

Even Bottom's ignorance makes us like him. When the exquisite queen of the fairies falls in love with him, adoring his looks and voice, he sees nothing incongruous: To him it seems like the most natural thing in the world, and why not? He is totally unaware of his lack of beauty, intelligence, or even ordinary common sense; his misplaced self-confidence is ludicrous.

Shakespeare's characters from the lower end of the social scale are nearly always marked by crude speech, poor grammar, comic illiteracy, and verbal blunders, especially malapropisms (misused big words). Shakespeare loves to poke gentle fun at their ignorance, and they rarely get things right when it is at all possible to get them wrong.

Part of Bottom's charm is that he is completely immune to romantic love. In this respect, he is the opposite of all the infatuated characters around him. He may be cruder and more stupid than they are, but he never gets carried away by his emotions. So when Titania pours out her love to him, he receives the news with perfect calm. He is polite but puzzled. Yet he has not the faintest curiosity about how this bizarre situation came to be!

Act III, Scene 2

Overview

Puck reports to Oberon, who is delighted to learn that the love-juice has made Titania fall in love with the absurd-looking Puck and, furthermore, has caused the disdainful youth to fall in love with poor Helena. But then Hermia and Demetrius enter, he begging her for love and she accusing him of murdering Lysander, which he denies. She angrily leaves him alone, and he lies down to sleep in despair.

Now Oberon and Puck realize that Puck has made a serious blunder, anointing the eyes of the wrong "Athenian youth" and causing him to fall for the wrong maiden. Oberon angrily orders Puck to go and fetch Helena at once. As soon as he is gone, Oberon applies the magic juice to Demetrius's eyes.

Puck returns a moment later, followed by Lysander and Helena, who are quarreling. He is insisting that he loves her; she refuses to believe it, and accuses him of mocking her. How, she asks, can he be so fickle as to abandon Hermia? "I had no judgment when to her I swore," he replies, adding that "Demetrius loves her, and he loves not you."

Amidst all of the other confusion,
Titania still regards Bottom lovingly.

Just then Demetrius wakes up, sees Helena, and makes extravagant professions of his love for her. Naturally, Helena assumes that both men are cruelly making fun of her! Lysander assumes Demetrius is making fun of Helena, too, and the two men argue bitterly as Hermia arrives. She accuses Lysander of abandoning her, and when he tells her that he now hates her and loves Helena, Helena becomes furious with her friend and concludes that all three of them have formed a "confederacy" to ridicule her. Hermia says she is amazed at this fury.

The uproar and confusion get worse until all four lovers stalk off, enraged. Oberon blames Puck for creating this unhappy situation and orders him to produce a fog over the forest and keep the men at odds by imitating their voices until all four lovers fall asleep. Then, Oberon tells Puck to use the magic juice to renew Lysander's love for Hermia. When the lovers awaken, all four will remember this whole night only as a dream.

Once everything has been straightened out, Oberon himself will go to Titania, beg her for the Indian boy, and break the spell that has made her infatuated with Bottom. All this must be accomplished before morning. Obeying Oberon's command, Puck taunts Lysander and Demetrius, separately goading them to fight until, unable to see in the fog, they lie down to sleep, exhausted. Then the two women return and fall asleep, too.

Analysis

It is in this scene that Puck makes his famous comment: "Lord, what fools these mortals be!" The lovers' behavior, especially that of the two young men, makes this statement hard to argue with. Under the influence of the magic juice, the lovers become spectacularly "inconstant"— that is, fickle and changeable. They vow eternal love one moment, but love turns into furious hate the next. And the best part of the joke is that they attribute their sudden and arbitrary changes of mood and mind to "reason" and "judgment." They see nothing ironic in their irrational passions.

But, of course, the same is true of Titania. All of this makes the stolid Bottom seem, by comparison, a model of emotional stability. And Bottom, in his way, agrees with Puck when he observes that "reason and love keep little company together nowadays." In the midsummer night's chaos of the woods, we nearly forget the pattern of mature love represented by Theseus and Hippolyta, where love and reason seem to keep company together.

We may recall Lysander's complaint in the first scene, another of the play's most familiar lines: "The course of true love never did run smooth." When he spoke these words, however, he was thinking of tragic external obstacles and enemies (such as those faced by Romeo and Juliet or Pyramus and Thisby), not the comically insane whims of the lovers' own hearts that this story will expose.

Act IV, Scene 1

Overview

As the four lovers slumber, Titania tenderly caresses Bottom and orders her fairies to bring him whatever he desires. With fine, formal courtesy he requests honey, hay, oats, and "a peck of provender"—a basket of feed. As for music, he reveals his crude, rustic taste by calling for simple musical instruments: "I have a reasonable good ear in music. Let's have the tongs and the bones." As Bottom and Titania doze off, Oberon, pitying his wife, decrees that the joke has gone far enough. Titania has also given him the Indian boy they were disputing. He tells Puck to restore Bottom's human head, while he himself breaks the spell on his queen.

Titania comes to, exclaiming that she has had a bad dream: "Methought I was enamor'd of an ass!" With a smile Oberon points to Bottom, who still has the ass's head: "There lies your love." It is time, he adds, for everyone to prepare for the great wedding in Athens. Puck restores Bottom's human head; Oberon calls for music, and all the fairies dance.

The Quarrel of Oberon and Titania
by Sir Joseph Noel Paton

When Bottom awakens, he thinks the entire episode was all a dream.

Hunting horns are heard, and Theseus arrives with Hippolyta, Egeus, and his court. Theseus and Hippolyta discuss the music made by their hounds' voices during a hunt. They discover the sleeping lovers, who then awaken. Lysander confesses that he and Hermia have come to the woods to escape the law of Athens, but before he can finish his statement, Egeus angrily interrupts him and demands that the law be brought against him in all its rigor.

Here, Demetrius interrupts to tell Theseus how he came into the woods in pursuit of Hermia, but strangely found himself ceasing to love her and passionately loving Helena instead. Hearing this, Theseus overrules Egeus and decrees that both pairs of lovers—Demetrius and Helena, Lysander and Hermia—shall be married with himself and Hippolyta in Athens. As the lovers are left together, they express bafflement at what has happened, and Demetrius speaks for all of them when he says: "Are you sure / That we are awake? It seems to me / That yet we sleep, we dream." Deciding that they are indeed awake, the four lovers follow Theseus and the others back to Athens, leaving the sleeping Bottom alone.

Yawning and opening his eyes, Bottom at first thinks he is rehearsing the play. Then he realizes he is alone and remembers his "vision," which he calls a "dream." He is overwhelmed by its profundity. Garbling a passage from the Bible, he says: "The eye of man hath not heard, the ear of man hath not seen, man's hand is not able to taste, his tongue to conceive, nor his heart to report what my dream was." Bottom decides that Peter Quince must write a ballad about this wondrous dream, which Bottom will sing at the end of the play.

Analysis

In this scene, all but one of the plot strands are tied up. The lovers are properly matched at last, the humane Theseus has overruled the tyrannical Egeus, Titania and Bottom are released from their spells, and everything is finally ready for the great wedding celebration we have been expecting since the play's very first lines.

Once again we see Bottom taking the most extraordinary events in stride and assuming command of Titania's fairies. His earthiness is hilariously incongruous with the enchanted atmosphere that surrounds him. We also hear of the strange harmony—the "musical discord" and "sweet thunder"—of Hippolyta's hounds' baying voices, which has been called a brilliant parallel to the blending of so many odd elements in *A Midsummer Night's Dream* itself: the legendary Greeks, the exquisite fairies, the country bumpkins.

Topping all this is Bottom's recollection of his "dream," or "vision." He thinks it was a revelation, and he describes it in a botched version of St. Paul's promise of heaven in the first (Biblical) letter to the Corinthians: "Eye hath not seen, nor ear heard, neither have entered into the heart of man, the things which God hath prepared for them that love him."

Act IV, Scene 2

Overview

The actors are in a tizzy. Bottom is missing! How can the play go on without the star?

Just then, Bottom shows up. Panic turns to great relief and joy. He instantly takes command of the situation. The play must proceed. He directs the actor who is playing the lion not to trim his nails, "for they shall hang out for the lion's claws." He says that the whole cast must "eat no onions nor garlic, for we are to utter sweet breath."

Analysis

This is the play's shortest scene, and it serves to prepare us for the grand climax of the final act. Once again, we see Bottom asserting his authority with his usual comic aplomb. Neither he nor his friends question his right to command. We have every reason to expect *Pyramus and Thisby* to be a disaster.

The scene illustrates a great comic principle: that a clever man dominating a dunce is never as funny as a dunce dominating another dunce—or a dunce dominating a clever man. Bottom's leadership of his foolish band, with unchallenged mastery, is one of Shakespeare's most inspired comic touches.

Bottom and his friends are so naïve, so free of any touch of malice, that they win our hearts; the more preposterous they are, the more we sympathize with them.

Act V, Scene 1

Overview

The great moment has arrived. The wedding festivities are in full swing. Theseus must choose an entertainment to fill the three hours between supper and bedtime.

Before he does so, however, he and Hippolyta discuss the strange story that the lovers have told them of the events in the woods. Theseus makes the following observation:

Lovers and madmen have such seething brains,
Such shaping fantasies, that apprehend
More than cool reason ever comprehends.
The lunatic, the lover, and the poet
Are of imagination all compact.
One sees more devils than vast hell can hold:
That is the madman. The lover, all as frantic,
Sees Helen's beauty in a brow of Egypt.
The poet's eye, in fine frenzy rolling,
Doth glance from heaven to earth,
from earth to heaven;
And as imagination bodies forth
The forms of things unknown, the poet's pen
Turns them to shapes, and gives to airy nothing
A local habitation and a name.

Philostrate, master of the revels, presents a list of four plays to choose from for the evening's amusement. Theseus rejects the first three but is attracted by the title of the fourth: "A tedious brief scene of young Pyramus and his love Thisby; very tragical mirth." Philostrate tries to dissuade Theseus from choosing that one; he has seen it rehearsed, and the poor workmen who acted it (Bottom and company) were so bad, he says, that he laughed until he cried.

That does it, and Theseus insists on *Pyramus and Thisby*. Philostrate protests that it would be cruel to make fun of the poor men; Hippolyta agrees with him. But Theseus replies that the true kindness to these men will be to accept their well-meaning offer. Their intentions matter more than their actual performance. Theseus is gracious enough to be pleased by their mere desire to please. As he explains to Hippolyta,

Our sport shall be to take what they mistake;
And what poor duty cannot do, noble respect
Takes it in might, not merit.
Where I have come, great clerks have purposed
To greet me with premeditated welcomes;
Where I have seen them shiver and look pale,
Make periods in the midst of sentences,
Throttle their practiced accent in their fears,
And, in conclusion, dumbly have broke off,
Not paying me a welcome. Trust me, sweet,
Out of this silence yet I pick'd a welcome,
And in the modesty of fearful duty
I read as much as from the rattling tongue
Of saucy and audacious eloquence.
Love, therefore, and tongue-tied simplicity
In least speak most, to my capacity.

We have to read this speech carefully several times to grasp its simple point: Theseus is saying that on occasions when great scholars ("clerks") have tried to greet him with well-rehearsed speeches, they were so nervous that they forgot their lines, but he appreciated their sincerity and overlooked their failure. In the same spirit, he will pardon the bumbling actors who are trying, however ineptly, to please the wedding party tonight.

And it is a good thing he takes this tolerant attitude, for the actors quickly prove that they need plenty of tolerance! Peter Quince delivers the play's prologue, misreading his lines (because he cannot even handle the punctuation properly) so that he actually reverses their meaning.

It gets worse. The actors playing Pyramus, Thisby, the lion, the moonshine, and the wall are so bad that the audience dissolves into laughter. Hippolyta calls the play "the silliest stuff that ever I heard."

Theseus wisely replies, "The best in this kind are but shadows, and the worst are no worse if imagination amend them." That is, even the best actors are only pretending, so if we use our imaginations, we can enjoy the worst just as well. Why complain? Enjoy the illusion!

And enjoy it the audience does, joking uproariously at the talking lion, the talking wall, and the talking moonshine. The play is a great success in spite of itself. After Pyramus and Thisby have stabbed themselves and died, the lion offers to deliver an epilogue, but Theseus assures him that this will be unnecessary. It is midnight, time for bed. After a brief dance, everyone retires for the night.

Puck enters to address the real audience, us. He delivers an eerily beautiful little rhyme about creatures of the night—the lion, wolf, screech owl, and ghosts released from their graves. Oberon, Titania, and the other fairies appear and all of them sing and dance until Oberon pronounces a solemn blessing on the married couples and the children they will have. Then everyone but Puck departs.

Puck apologizes for the play, asking our pardon "if we shadows have offended" and promising to make amends. After all it has been only a "dream." He begs our applause and bids us good night.

Analysis

Act V is the grand finale of Shakespeare's sweetest comedy, his least dramatic drama, his most joyous, and, some have even said, his greatest work of all. It brings together

Actors portraying the role of the wall in *Pyramus and Thisby*

nearly all the main characters; only Egeus, the tyrannical father who threatened the lovers' happiness, is missing. The wise and humane Theseus is fully in command of the human world.

Theseus opens the act with his famous speech disparaging imagination as the faculty that marks "the lunatic, the lover, and the poet." Yet, moments later, to excuse the poor actors, he notes that they are no worse than the best actors "if imagination"—that is, the audience's imagination—"amend them." He judges them with mercy. Reason, justice, love, and imagination, at odds throughout the play, are finally harmonized.

We also see in this act the emphasis on the power of the imagination. Theseus reminds the audience that "imagination bodies forth" under the "poet's pen," and in doing so, "gives to airy nothing / A local habitation and a name." As much as love and dreams have been subjects in *A Midsummer Night's Dream*, the repeated emphasis on imagination also gives insight into Shakespeare's focus on the subject itself. While Shakespeare's supreme tragedies are justly renowned for their profound studies of human character and fate, *A Midsummer Night's Dream* displays his genius in a different way.

If we go to this play expecting the excellences of those tragedies, we will only be disappointed and baffled. The story hardly matters; the characters seem trivial, almost interchangeable; what predominates is the mood of total enchantment in which anything can happen. The key terms and symbols are "love," "strange," "mad," "moon," and, of course, "dream."

The tragedy *A Midsummer Night's Dream* most resembles and sometimes reminds us of is *Romeo and Juliet*, and

Puck is characterized by his mischief and playfulness.

Lysander puts us in mind of that tragedy in the opening scene when he offers the moral that "the course of true love never did run smooth." But this world-famous observation turns out to be a joke, foreshadowing the very opposite of tragedy. Lysander, whose heart veers suddenly from Hermia to Helena and back to Hermia again, stands for anything but "true love." His love is fickleness itself, the plaything of Puck and the magic flower. There is a terrible logic of doom in a play like *Macbeth*, where every step the hero takes leads to his damnation, but in this play, all the events are light and arbitrary, and damnation seems impossible. In *Macbeth*, the hero is the villain; in this comedy, there are no villains, and villainy itself can hardly exist. The worst mischief is Puck's playful meddling.

It is because there is so little real suspense in *A Midsummer Night's Dream* that it has the permanent, even eternal, quality of myth: we remember its supernatural atmosphere, and especially the incident involving Bottom and Titania, long after we have lost any curiosity about how the very slight story will turn out. Since much of the story occurs at night with various characters under a spell, there is an overarching sense of the dream. And by the time we come to an end with Theseus's speeches, we remember how much this play is about love and the imagination.

List of Characters

Noble Characters

- Theseus: Duke of Athens
- Hippolyta: Queen of the Amazons and bride of Theseus

Edward Robert Hughes's *Midsummer Eve*

- Egeus: An Athenian nobleman, father of Hermia
- Lysander: Lover of Hermia
- Demetrius: Suitor of Hermia, approved by Egeus
- Philostrate: Theseus's master of the revels
- Hermia: Daughter of Egeus, in love with Lysander
- Helena: In love with Demetrius

Fairies

- Oberon: King of the fairies
- Titania: Queen of the fairies
- Puck (Robin Goodfellow): Fairy
- Peaseblossom, Cobweb, Moth, Mustardseed:
Minor fairies

Tradesmen (Actors)

- Peter Quince: A carpenter
- Nick Bottom: A weaver
- Francis Flute: A bellows-mender
- Tom Snout: A tinker
- Snug: A joiner
- Robin Starveling: A tailor

Analysis of Major Characters

The characters of *A Midsummer Night's Dream*, unlike those of Shakespeare's tragedies, offer us less to analyze than the characters in some of his other plays. Whole books have been written about Hamlet alone, but less is found on Puck or Bottom the Weaver. This doesn't mean that these characters aren't vital to the play itself, but their role in this comedy functions differently than the role of Shakespeare's characters in his tragedies.

In many ways, there are not any lead roles in the play, but rather numerous supporting roles.

Theseus

Theseus seems, at first glance, to be the most important character in the play, the wise and reasonable ruler of Athens. The others appeal to him to settle their disputes; he has a commanding presence yet is sensitive in handling the problems presented to him. At his climactic wedding, he graciously accepts the tradesmen's bungling attempt to please him with their preposterous play and is sympathetic towards them.

Hippolyta

Hippolyta, Theseus's bride, is queen of the Amazons, legendary warrior women, but she shows no ferocity here; rather, she is a highly civilized and sympathetic figure who speaks very few words.

The Four Lovers

Lysander, Demetrius, Hermia, and Helena have so little individuality that we can barely tell them apart. And this is surely deliberate on Shakespeare's part, since he is unsurpassed at creating characters of the greatest depth and complexity when he wants to. In this play, he is doing something utterly different from what he does in his tragedies, where the plots are driven by human choice, and character is fate. Here fate is magical and whimsical, and the fairies are in control. Rounded, three-dimensional figures would be out of place and would destroy the spell of the poetry.

Oberon

Oberon is king of the fairies and a very different ruler than Theseus. Oberon can be nearly as silly as the human lovers and is inclined to petulance and immaturity in his desire to get what he wants. While he is capable of having sympathy and rationality, these characteristics in him are on shallow display.

Titania

Titania is the fairy queen and the focus of Oberon's frustration; she is subjected to his magical manipulation yet by play's end has re-emerged as a fully empowered queen.

Puck (also known as Robin Goodfellow)

Puck is Oberon's mischievous lieutenant, and at Oberon's commanding, he performs pranks and casts charms on the humans. This character also manages to speak some of Shakespeare's simplest and most exquisite verse—of bats, owls, spiders, crabs, geese, worms, larks, mice, serpents, cowslips, acorns, and other homely natural things. More than any other character, he creates the play's atmosphere of night and enchantment.

Bottom the Weaver

Bottom the Weaver steals the show, though not in the way he intends to. He has absolutely no sense of the magical and supernatural forces around him. Stolid and practical, he remains completely unaware of his own transformation into an ass. When Puck restores his human head and releases Titania from the spell of the flower's juice, Bottom thinks he has had an amazing "vision" in a dream. He is totally immune to love; he believes he is a great actor who will move the courtly audience to deep emotion. His ignorance is obvious to everyone but him and his equally obtuse friends, who admire him greatly. In a sense, Bottom's invincible self-image is the biggest joke of the play! When the story, the poetry, and the other characters bewitch us, he brings us back to earthy reality.

And yet, Shakespeare lets this clown have the most profound insight into love and imagination, when he awakens to speak of his "most rare vision." Among all Shakespeare's comic characters, only *Henry IV*'s Falstaff rivals Bottom. It is hard to say which of the two is the greater comic giant.

 *Chapter Three*

A Closer Look

In addition to *A Midsummer Night's Dream* showing off some of Shakespeare's most stunning poetry, the play offers readers and audiences some favorite themes and intriguing motifs and symbols, leading to varied interpretations. These themes, which largely relate to love and identity, are arguably present in some of his other plays but do not have the particular look present here; perhaps that is because Shakespeare transforms them through the wilder and more fantastical forms that are at work in *A Midsummer Night's Dream.* Despite how silly or ridiculous the play may seem at times, we know that much more is at stake for Shakespeare. Whether it is in the realms of romantic relationships, philosophies about the nature of reality or identity, the complexities of religion, or the layers of social orders, we have much to learn about the past and present from this play.

Themes

Love's Irrationality

One of the chief themes of *A Midsummer Night's Dream*, to put it very prosaically, is that love is irrational. Poets and lovers may talk about true love, but in this play, love is utterly whimsical, at the mercy of fairies and flowers. The lovers may delude themselves into thinking that their love is the product of reason and can never change; we know better. We see Lysander pledge his eternal devotion to Hermia, and then, awaking after Puck has anointed his eyes with fairy juice, abruptly switch his affections to Helena, with this comical explanation:

> *Not Hermia, but Helena I love.*
> *Who will not change a raven for a dove?*
> *The will of man is by his reason sway'd,*
> *And reason says you are the worthier maid.*

Obviously reason has nothing to do with it. No wonder Helena thinks Lysander is making a cruel joke of her. Her suspicion is doubled when Demetrius, who has threatened to kill or violate her, also pours out his love: "O Helen, goddess, nymph, perfect, divine!" Then she thinks Hermia has also joined the two men in a conspiracy (or "confederacy") to mock her. Mockery, however, is not the final note of the play, and by play's end, the lovers have been returned to their right relationships.

Further evidence for the theme of love's irrationality can be found in the lines spoken between the characters of Bottom and Titania. Due to being under a magical spell, Titania hears Bottom's voice and then proclaims:

Mine ear is much enamored of thy note.
So is mine eye enthralled to thy shape.
And thy fair virtue's force perforce doth move me
On the first view to say, to swear, I love thee.

In response to her surprising affections, Bottom says,

Methinks, mistress, you should have little reason for that.
And yet, to say the truth, reason and love keep little
company together
Nowadays.

The fact that Titania's confession of love (not the first one in the play!) occurs while she is under a spell speaks to this sense of love's irrationality; furthermore, Bottom is viewed as the most ignorant character in the play, so for him to be the one to speak of "reason" (while appearing as an ass) adds more comedic effect and further drives home the theme of love's irrationality.

Reality Versus Fantasy

One of the first clues that fantasy is at work in an overt way in this play is through the title itself. Furthermore, one of the plot strands of the fairies' involvement with the human world is more evidence of this theme. Yet even in the human world, the desires of the character of Bottom speak to fantasy.

While the play begins in the world of humans around the plot of the marriage of Theseus and Hippolyta, the play as a whole is not about the fulfillment of this marriage, nor is it just about the outcome of the other young lovers' relationships. The reality of the relationships is affected by the world of the fairies. The discord in the fairy realm leads to the integration of magic into the reality of the human world; this blurring leads to various fantastical enactments. We see for a brief time the fantasy of Helena come to life when Lysander has been affected by fairy juice; we also see the clownish Bottom not only temporarily transformed into an ass, but also become the brief object of Titania's affections.

Outside of the enchanted realm of the forest, there is another way that fantasy is at work in reality. Bottom's desires to put on a successful play for the wedding speak to this. Bottom and his cast of fellow tradesmen are not fully prepared for handling the play, yet he has visions of grandiosity about his own abilities as an actor. In this instance in particular, perhaps Shakespeare was speaking to the ways in which we all may suffer a fantasy, at times, about our own abilities.

Finally, some critics argue that the play itself operates on the level of being a fantasy, or dream, of one of the characters. Some argue that it is Bottom's dream and that the following lines speak to this interpretation:

> *I have had a most rare vision. I have had a dream, past the wit of man to say what dream it was. Man is but an ass, if he go about to expound this dream. Methought I was— there is no man can tell what. Methought I was—and methought I had—but man is but a patch'd fool, if he will offer to say what methought I had.*

Bottom speaks with the difficulty—especially if one struggles with language—of someone waking from a dream and trying to articulate its content and meaning.

Others argue that if the play is meant to be received as a fantasy or dream then it is the audience's, as Puck's epilogue tells us:

If we shadows have offended,
Think but this, and all is mended,
That you have but slumbered here
While these visions did appear.

Whether the play represents the audience's dream or Bottom's or neither, it is clear that Shakespeare wanted to emphasize some of the ways in which fantasy and dreams intermingle with reality.

Instability of Identity

As previously mentioned, some of the characters' lives are altered temporarily in the play. Despite the fact that this altering occurs by the magical work of the fairies, the characters' sense of their own identity shifts for a time. Much of our understanding of each of the characters of the young lovers—Hermia and Helena, Lysander and Demetrius—relies on their romantic attachment of who is pursuing whom. Through the work of interfering Puck, the object of their affections changes. This also happens to Titania and perhaps represents the most drastic of alterations, as she briefly loves the transformed Bottom. With these shifts in identity—even if through the form of an outside force—we gain a sense of the chaos that ensues when an important sense of self is disrupted. Some critics contend that because of so many of these shifts, especially in the realm of love relationships, Shakespeare was drawing attention to the instability of identity, or perhaps to the illusion of its stability.

A further example of this instability of identity exits in the character of Bottom. We do not see a change in him in the realm of romantic attachment since this character seems to not have any object of romantic affection, but rather, he is a character who wants to embody multiple characters in the play within the play; in this regard, he may serve as a reminder of the various roles individuals pursue, forgoing any singular identity.

The Value of Imagination and Art

Related to the themes of love, instability of identity, and reality versus fantasy is the theme of the value of imagination and art. Shakespeare draws attention to the role of imagination through fantasy, both in the world of the fairies and in the various ways that love is represented. Shakespeare even has some of the characters speak directly at times to the role of imagination; let's return to this important passage to emphasize the theme:

> *Lovers and madmen have such seething brains,*
> *Such shaping fantasies, that apprehend*
> *More than cool reason ever comprehends.*
> *The lunatic, the lover, and the poet*
> *Are of imagination all compact.*
> *One sees more devils than vast hell can hold:*
> *That is the madman. The lover, all as frantic,*
> *Sees Helen's beauty in a brow of Egypt.*
> *The poet's eye, in fine frenzy rolling,*
> *Doth glance from heaven to earth,*
> *from earth to heaven;*
> *And as imagination bodies forth*
> *The forms of things unknown, the poet's pen*
> *Turns them to shapes, and gives to airy nothing*
> *A local habitation and a name.*

Imagination is tied not only to love and to the "lover" but also to the "poet," or artist.

The value of art (even when fraught with complexity and difficulty) is also at work through the play within the play. Despite the problems with the tradesmen's production of the play *Pyramus and Thisby*, the show goes on and overall receives a warm reception. Shakespeare uses Theseus's response to the play, "The best in this kind are but shadows, and the worst are no worse if imagination amend them" to suggest that the audience itself has an important role in how it relates to and "amend[s]" art; the audience is invited to join the laughter of the very real blundering of the tradesmen putting together the play. By doing so, Shakespeare demonstrates to the *Midsummer Night's Dream* audience the power of theater to suspend reality; at the same time, it is a reminder that despite our very real foibles and blunders in life, we can laugh.

Motifs

A Midsummer Night's Dream is marked by dizzying repetition of interrelated key words, many of them contrasting (or ambiguously related to each other): dreaming and waking, sleep and death, eyes and blindness, moon and light, night and day, magic and music, songs and shrieks, tears and laughter, wisdom and folly, judgment and imagination, Venus and Cupid, comedy and tragedy, sport and illusion, love and hate, love and law, love and reason. Used countless times, they set a definite tone, but they also keep us confused and off balance. The elements are simple, yet too abundant for us to grasp fully—"more than cool reason ever comprehends," like dreams within a dream. Our minds are overwhelmed—as Shakespeare means them to be. He never intended his audience to take it all in. Our confusion is the very effect he intended when he wrote the play; we should never feel stupid for being confused.

In all of Shakespeare's plays—we can never repeat this too often—Shakespeare's language is deliberately too dense for easy understanding. We only glimpse his full meaning. Each rereading yields us fuller glimpses of a play's real depth. No simple paraphrase or translation can possibly give us all of it, and the volumes of books written about the plays should remind us of this fact. Is Shakespeare's work confusing? Of course. It is supposed to be. Shakespeare makes us laugh at our own confusion.

Like many of Shakespeare's comedies, this one moves from the "normal" world (Athens, in this case—the realm of law, order, and reason), to an enchanted one (the nocturnal forest ruled by the fairies), then back to the normal one (where magic becomes the marriage festivity). Which one is the real world? Even this is left in doubt at the end, when Puck tells us that the whole story has been a dream!

We may compare *A Midsummer Night's Dream* to *As You Like It*, which begins in the normal court world, moves to the enchanted Forest of Arden (where the love story occurs and the characters are transformed, though without magic), and back to the world of the court; and *The Tempest*, where the whole story takes place on an enchanted island—though we learn that the action really began back in Milan, Italy, the "normal" world, where, at the story's end, the transformed characters will return to normal life, leaving magic behind. (There is even a figure like Puck, the sexless spirit Ariel, who obeys the

Shakespeare's plays often blend the natural and the supernatural.

magician-hero Prospero, in whom Shakespeare seems to combine Oberon and Theseus.)

Other Shakespearean comedies follow the same pattern, whether supernatural action is overt, merely implied, or faintly suggested by the outline of the story. Some are as realistic as *The Two Gentlemen of Verona*, some as otherworldly as *The Winter's Tale*. Even in a play with the realism of *The Two Gentlemen of Verona*, we still have instances of mistaken identity, mischievous behavior, and characters in disguise. Shakespeare's comedies, with all their rich variations, display the astounding versatility of his genius. How could a single imagination create so much? "After God," one critic has marveled, "Shakespeare has created most." Yet he never simply repeats a successful formula; each of his masterpieces is something totally, miraculously new.

Shakespeare's tragedies observe a similar pattern, from normal to abnormal and back again. In *Hamlet*, for example, a mysterious ghost in armor, looking like the late King Hamlet and accompanied by feverish preparations for war, interrupts the peaceful life of Denmark; then we see the royal court of the new king, unaware of this strange eruption. The ghost tells Prince Hamlet a terrible secret, and the real story begins. After much violence and intrigue, Denmark seems to return to normal, only to explode in a final scene of violence and death. Then Norway conquers Denmark, and the tragedy ends in real peace.

Even *King Lear*, the darkest of Shakespeare's tragedies, follows something like this comic outline. The action begins at Lear's apparently normal court, where he tries, foolishly, to divide his kingdom peacefully among his three daughters, two of whom despise him. When this scheme results in chaos, with the banishment of his only true-hearted daughter, Cordelia, and the faithful earl of Kent, he is forced to flee to the wilderness with his fool, where he goes mad and is transformed by suffering into a wiser man. After his terrible ordeal, which ends in death, the play returns to a desolate normality, in which it ends.

And in *Lear* too, Shakespeare's language, for the most part, is deliberately complex; it is simplest only in the most crucial and emotional scenes. The tremendous, heart-rending scene in which Lear and Cordelia are reunited is written in some of the plainest words he ever wrote: "You do me wrong to take me out of the grave... I know you do not love me ..." The same is true when Othello says, "My heart is turned to stone. I strike it, and it hurts my hand ... But yet the pity of it, Iago! O Iago, the pity of it, Iago!" (One reason for Shakespeare's many songs, especially in the comedies, is to clarify and intensify his emotional meaning as much as possible.) And, of course, Hamlet speaks the simplest and most famous sentence in the English language: "To be or not to be: that is the question."

Symbols

The Characters

In *A Midsummer Night's Dream*, the characters themselves are hardly more than symbols. Theseus represents human rationality and the ideal of civility; the four nearly identical lovers stand for the folly and fickleness of love; Puck stands for the playful whimsy of Fairyland; and Bottom stands for innocent and lovable stupidity. Venus, of course, is the goddess of love; her son Cupid symbolizes love's arbitrary randomness. Phoebe, goddess of the moon, governs the earth's waters, which also represent both purification and change.

The Moon

References to the moon occur throughout *A Midsummer Night's Dream*. Not only do the references help establish a sense of time in the play, but they also take on another meaning that some members of the Elizabethan audience would've known. In particular, there is reference to both the old moon and the new moon as well as to the goddess Diana, who represented both celibacy and chaste love.

Language

If Shakespeare seems hard for us to read without plenty of footnotes, we should always bear in mind that he would need far more footnotes to read modern English than we need to read him. He would find us baffling. We must beware of the assumption that his language merely reflects the way English people spoke spontaneously "in those days." It does not. Shakespeare's language sounds "artificial" to our modern ears, and that is for a very good reason: It *is* artificial. It is deliberately artificial.

And right at the beginning, if we want to understand Shakespeare at all, we must get rid of a very silly modern prejudice: the notion that art should always be "natural" and that whatever is artificial is phony. The very words "art" and "artificial" (along with "artifice" and others) are obviously related.

In *The Adventures of Huckleberry Finn*, a comic masterpiece in its own right—though vastly different from *A Midsummer Night's Dream*—Mark Twain has immense fun with the way Shakespeare sounded to illiterate people on the American frontier. The fraudulent "duke" whom Huck and Jim encounter on the Mississippi River plans to make a fortune by presenting bogus productions of Shakespeare to the local rubes, featuring a mangled version of Hamlet's soliloquy. He patches together famous lines from the tragedies, not realizing that he has completely misunderstood them. (Huck doesn't understand them, either; he takes everything quite seriously.) The "duke" is nearly as ignorant as his intended victims.

Shakespeare's formal English is a foreign language to Twain's yokels. Twain's ultimate joke, a sophisticated one, is that these yokels are overawed by genuinely literary language; they understand only crudely plain and practical English, and they mistake anything else for refined eloquence, no matter how absurd it may be. All the characters in *Huckleberry Finn*, you might say, exist on the same intellectual level as Bottom the Weaver. They are completely unprepared for real art, which is artificial.

It is impossible, by definition, for art *not* to be artificial. Even lyrics of rap music are artificial. After all, they rhyme. They may seem "natural" when compared with the lyrics of the old songs of Broadway musicals, but this is only relative. Rhyme and fixed rhythms are a highly unnatural form of expression, so even the difference between rap and grand opera is, in the end, merely a matter of degree. The so-called realism we usually prefer is just a matter of taste; we expect art to stress its realism and to conceal, as much as possible, its artifice.

Consider a classic movie like *The Godfather*. When it was released in 1972, it seemed like the ultimate in realism, with its violence, its raw language, its breaking of old taboos, and various other shocking departures from the conventions of older gangster films. Suddenly, everything before it seemed quaint; at the time, it was the most exciting film ever made—but only for a while. It was followed by far more graphic gangster films (such as *Goodfellas*, for example) that now make it, in turn, seem rather quaint and artificial to today's audiences. The original shock is gone.

This may be a good place to emphasize our earlier point. If Shakespeare could see *The Godfather*, he would need a huge book, many times longer than this one, to make it comprehensible to him. He knew nothing of a thousand details that we take for granted: inventions such as the automobile and the electric light, historical events such as World War II (or even the existence of New York City, with all its immigrant groups), not to mention all the technology of motion pictures (with everything from photography to sound recording); he would also be a little puzzled by common expressions such as *high-tech*, *feel the heat*, *approval ratings*, *war criminal*, *judgmental*, *hash tags*, and *social media*. The list of words and concepts, after four centuries, is endless.

Given this vast difference between Shakespeare's world and language and ours, how can we call him "the greatest master of the English language"? It might seem as if he barely spoke English at all! The words of Shakespeare's time have also become archaic. Words like "thou," "thee," "thy," "thyself," and "thine," which were among the most common words in the language in Shakespeare's day, have all but disappeared today. We simply say "you" for both singular and plural, formal and familiar. Most other modern languages have kept their version of "thou." Sometimes the same words now have different meanings. We are apt to be misled by such simple, familiar words as "kind," "wonderful," "waste," "just," and "dear," which he often uses in ways that differ from our usage. Shakespeare also doesn't always use the words we expect to hear, the words that we ourselves would naturally use. When we might automatically say, "I beg your pardon" or just "Sorry," he might say, "I cry you mercy."

But as emphasized before, it is most important to bear in mind that Shakespeare was often hard for his first audiences to understand. Even in his own time, his rich language was challenging. And this was deliberate. Shakespeare was inventing his own kind of English; it was indeed a successful invention when taking into consideration the way his words and phrases have stayed with us, even in everyday usage.

It is Shakespeare's mastery of the English language that keeps his words familiar to us today. Many of his dramatic lines are commonly known: "Wherefore art thou Romeo?"; "My kingdom for a horse!"; "To be or not to be: that is the question"; "Friends, Romans, countrymen, lend me your ears"; and "What fools these mortals be!" Shakespeare's sonnets are also quoted on a regular basis and are noted for their sweetness: "Shall I compare thee to a summer's day?"

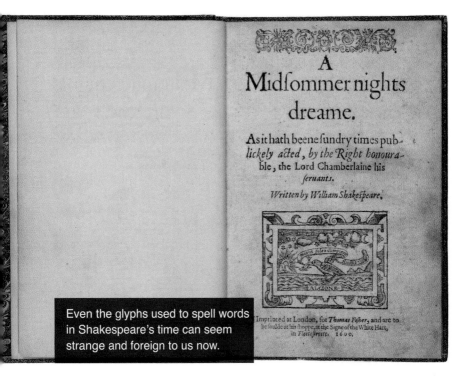

A

Midfommer nights

dreame.

As it hath beene fundry times pub-
lickely acted, by the Right honoura-
ble, the Lord Chamberlaine his
feruants.

Written by William Shakespeare.

Imprinted at London, for Thomas Fisher, and are to
be foulde at his fhoppe, at the Signe of the White Hart,
in Fleetefreete. 1600.

Even the glyphs used to spell words in Shakespeare's time can seem strange and foreign to us now.

Shakespeare's vocabulary was huge, full of references to the Bible as well as Greek and Roman mythology. Yet his most brilliant phrases often combine very simple and familiar words: "What's in a name? That which we call a rose / By any other name would smell as sweet." Hundreds of phrases have entered the English language from *Hamlet* alone, including "to hold, as t'were, the mirror up to nature"; "murder most foul"; "the thousand natural shocks that flesh is heir to"; "flaming youth"; "a countenance more in sorrow than in anger"; "the play's the thing"; "neither a borrower nor a lender be"; "in my mind's eye"; "something is rotten in the state of Denmark"; "alas, poor Yorick"; and "the lady doth protest too much, methinks."

From other plays we get the phrases "star-crossed lovers"; "we have scotched the snake, not killed it"; "one fell swoop"; "it was Greek to me;" "I come to bury Caesar, not to praise him"; and "the most unkindest cut of all"—all these are among our household phrases. In fact, Shakespeare even gave us the expression "household words." No wonder his contemporaries marveled at his "fine filed phrase" and swooned at the "mellifluous and honey-tongued Shakespeare."

Shakespeare's words seem to combine music, magic, wisdom, and humor: "The course of true love never did run smooth"; "The fault, dear Brutus, is not in our stars, But in ourselves, that we are underlings"; "Cowards die many times before their deaths; The valiant never taste of death but once"; "Not that I loved Caesar less, but that I loved Rome more"; "There are more things in heaven and earth, Horatio, than are dreamt of in your philosophy"; "Brevity is the soul of wit"; "There's a divinity that shapes our ends, Rough hew them how we will." The list of his words and phrases that continue to be used could go on and on.

The English language, of course, has changed almost beyond recognition since the time in which Shakespeare was writing, and the world has become enormously more complex. When returning to the idea that Shakespeare's own vocabulary and style were never easy for audiences to grasp and that he never meant them to be, this is where the role of artificiality becomes so important; Shakespeare wrote in a consciously heightened style that was unlike everyday speech. Most of his characters speak in blank verse—lines of ten syllables, usually unrhymed—while some speak in rhyme. Others, especially low characters like Bottom and his friends, speak in prose, which may be comically illiterate, but even this is artificial and far from the way people actually talked in normal conversation.

In *A Midsummer Night's Dream*, Shakespeare also created imaginary styles of expression that were suitable to the imaginary world and the fantastic characters he was creating. Theseus, Puck, and Bottom are all equally "unnatural" in their different ways, just as the fantastic characters in Mozart's great opera *The Magic Flute* all sing in styles that are appropriate both to themselves and to the work as a whole. Like Shakespeare's comedy, Mozart's opera is about enchantment (its French title is *La Flûte Enchantée*).

In contrast to the overtly imaginary world created in plays, movies almost demand realism. Other art forms, however, such as ballet, have their roots in ritual and virtually require a more formal approach. Attempts to make opera naturalistic, for example, have usually failed. If your taste in the performing arts runs to gritty film noir, you are unlikely to care for slapstick comedy. Such forms are equally stylized, but they cannot be combined.

Finally, we may ask why tragedy is supposed to be more real—and realistic—than comedy. Are tears more true to life than laughter? Is the morbid preferable to the ordinary, the nonexistent more fundamental than the actual? Is grief more basic than joy? And is death more "real" than life? Obviously the answer to all these questions is no. It can never be yes. So why has the dark and tragic in art—the "realistic"—become more prestigious than the bright, the joyful, the comic?

Shakespeare's Influence on Music

SHAKESPEARE'S WORK HAS had tremendous influence on other art forms, including music. The Bard has inspired composers of classical music for centuries, but even in contemporary popular music, his presence can be found.

One of the most renowned musicians and songwriters of the twentieth century, Bob Dylan, pays tribute to Shakespeare on his album *Highway 61 Revisited*, released in 1965, with his song "Desolation Row." In the song lyrics, Dylan references two tragic Shakespearean characters—Romeo from *Romeo and Juliet* and Ophelia from *Hamlet*. Dylan writes of Ophelia, "Her sin is her lifelessness / And though her eyes are fixed upon / Noah's great rainbow / She spends her time peeking / Into Desolation Row." While the song alludes to various figures in history, this reference speaks to the suicide of the young woman, echoing some of the themes of chaos and loss in the song.

The character of Ophelia has influenced many other musicians, including the singer and songwriter Natalie Merchant. Merchant's 1998 album is titled *Ophelia,* and the title song refers to the tragic character. Beyond this, however, the album also reimagines the character of Ophelia as representing many female archetypes.

Another iconic musician of the 1960s, John Lennon, found inspiration from Shakespeare for the Beatles' song "I Am the Walrus." After overhearing a dramatic reading of *King Lear* on BBC radio, Lennon decided to incorporate some of the lines of

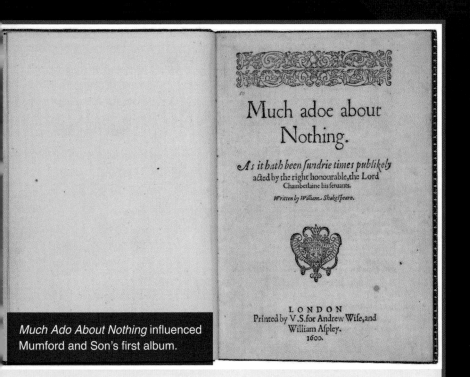

Much Ado About Nothing influenced Mumford and Son's first album.

the play into the song. Lines from *King Lear* can be heard, though somewhat garbled, in various versions of the song.

Lines from Shakespeare's *Much Ado About Nothing* are at work in the band Mumford and Son's first album, *Sigh No More*. The title song refers to the line, "Sigh no more, ladies, sigh no more" as sung by the character of Balthasar in the play. While this may be the most obvious nod to Shakespeare in the band's first album, it certainly is not the only one!

A Midsummer Night's Dream has been staged as a ballet, merging the play's comedy and the formality of ballet.

One possible practical reason is that tragedy focuses on the individual, while comedy is concerned with the entire society, so that the tragic actor receives more attention, fame, and glory than any group or ensemble of performers. At any rate, Shakespeare shows the most total command of both modes, tragic and comic. Neither is necessarily more "natural" than the other. Shakespeare blended them brilliantly, and his contemporaries praised him as an excellent "imitator of nature."

Interpreting the Play

Shakespearean Comedy

A Midsummer Night's Dream is, in a sense, Shakespeare's purest comedy. According to an old and stubborn idea, Shakespeare wrote comedies when he was in a happy mood and tragedies when he was in a more somber frame of mind, entering a "tragic period" during a time of personal troubles. One critic rightly ridiculed this notion under the heading of "the mythical sorrows of Shakespeare."

Today most scholars agree that Shakespeare was an artist whose works may not correspond at all to his personal feelings when he wrote them. An architect may design a mansion or a cathedral, but which he chooses to do probably has nothing to do with whether he is in a religious mood when he decides. It may be simply a matter of which he has been asked or hired to do.

A Midsummer Night's Dream, for all we know, may have been written for an important wedding celebration. We have too little information to settle the question, and we have no reason to answer it anyway. All we need to know is that Shakespeare wrote both comedies and tragedies, as well as history plays, and in many cases his plays are hard to classify. Shakespeare was always ready to mix genres, sometimes blending history, comedy, *and* tragedy in the same play.

In his *Poetics*, an important work of literary criticism, Aristotle described a tragedy as a play that moves an audience to feel "pity and fear" for the sufferings of its chief characters, who should be noble but imperfect figures whose flaws bring disaster on themselves. This little book had an enormous influence on Renaissance Europe, but whether it directly influenced Shakespeare is another unanswerable question. In any case Aristotle's preference for strict unity of plot and tone certainly failed to prevent the English playwright from combining tragedy with other elements. Followers of Aristotle often attacked Shakespeare for violating the Greek's prescriptions; many French critics even considered him vulgar!

The truth is that Shakespeare cares nothing for "unity" in the negative and narrow sense. He loves variety: the rich cast of characters, the opulent vocabulary, the complex plot, sudden alternations of tears and laughter, wild rhetoric, constant surprise. He seems to mock every notion of "rules" of drama. No playwright remotely like him, ancient or modern, had ever existed before. None has existed since. It seems safe to predict that none ever will.

No two of his plays are alike. He almost never repeated himself. Although his tragedies can be rich in humor, his comedies likewise contain much pathos, loss, and death. G. K. Chesterton, in a fine appreciation of *A Midsummer Night's Dream*, summed up its spirit in one inspired phrase: "the

Contemporary interpretations of Shakespeare's *A Midsummer Night's Dream* bring new meanings and layers to the work.

mysticism of happiness." He added: "In pure poetry and the intoxication of words, Shakespeare never rose higher than he rises in this play." The whole play captures the atmosphere of an "exasperating dream," where nothing quite makes sense and every explanation only deepens the mystery. The plot is a labyrinth.

In contrast to Shakespeare's tragedies, the atmosphere of *A Midsummer Night's Dream* is more important than the characters, who, except for Bottom, we hardly remember at all. None of them is serious in the way that Hamlet, Romeo, or even the heroes and heroines of the other great comedies are serious. It is no use analyzing them as if they were three-dimensional figures. We can hardly imagine them existing outside this play, or populating other plays. They belong here and nowhere else. They live only because the play lives. Like the dream it is, *A Midsummer Night's Dream* could never have a sequel!

Order and Chaos

Though Shakespeare's personal attitudes are often hard to identify, we can safely say that he loves order, harmony, music, and festivity. In that respect, he is deeply conservative. He rejoices in the normal, the happy, in love, marriage, and childbirth. His plays are full of songs and dances, which are easy to overlook when we read them on the page. In none of his plays are music, songs, rhyme, dancing, and theater so dominant as in *A Midsummer Night's Dream*, where love really does conquer all under Puck's benign magic spells. Even Bottom rejoices in the arts, taking hilarious pride in his supposed gifts for acting and music.

His villains and troublemakers dislike these things. Egeus, in *A Midsummer Night's Dream*, demands his own daughter's death when she refuses to marry Demetrius, the man he has chosen for her. When the lovers triumph in spite of him, he vanishes from the play and is absent from the great wedding revels in the final act. It is hard to imagine Egeus enjoying Bottom's performance as Pyramus!

Generalizations about Shakespeare are usually risky, but he has no fondness for malcontents, either those who rigidly defend an old order or those who would damage or overturn it. Egeus is somewhat unusual in that he carries attachment to an old law to such an extreme that he becomes the play's malcontent.

In Shakespeare, there is always a sense that the world used to be better, that preventing its getting worse is the best we can hope for, and that there is no such thing as progress in the modern sense. Because of the world's natural tendency to worsen, to dissolve into chaos, with rightful kings often displaced by usurping tyrants, we must learn to be content with what we have. In Oberon and, especially, Puck, Shakespeare presents supernatural powers not as dark and ominous, but as positive, kindly, and humorous forces. The world is full of bad omens threatening chaos—storms, eclipses, wars, ghosts, witches, and prophecies—but we can preserve our most joyful experiences in festivities, celebration, music, drama, and the arts.

Nevertheless, Shakespeare's world is basically a happy one. If it seldom makes progress in our sense, if it is forever threatened by the abnormal, it also has a natural tendency to recover from tragedy and return to normal. Beauty may be temporarily destroyed by raw power, but it is always reborn. *A Midsummer Night's Dream* expresses the poet's sheer love of the normal more ecstatically than anything else he ever wrote. No wonder it has remained one of his most popular plays, inspiring other works of genius, such as Felix Mendelssohn's glorious incidental music.

A Catholic Angle?

Until now, most scholars have assumed that Shakespeare had little to say about the events of his own time; in their view, he stayed carefully aloof from the raging political and religious disputes of his day and kept his opinions, if he had any, to himself. He was "universal," but only in a negative way, commenting on human nature but seldom if ever taking sides in the notable contemporary controversies that were splitting Elizabethan England and spilling much blood.

In 2005, Clare Asquith boldly challenged this view, expressed in all previous Shakespeare studies, in her amazing book *Shadowplay: The Hidden Beliefs and Coded Politics of William Shakespeare*. If her controversial thesis is widely accepted, we will have to adopt a truly revolutionary new approach to the Bard. Asquith is far from the first to detect Catholic sympathies in the great dramatist; G. K. Chesterton and many others have done so before her, but she has taken this idea further than anyone else.

In her view, Shakespeare was definitely a passionate Catholic, but, fearing persecution by the Tudor regime, which exerted tight censorship over the press and theater (the only media of his time), was forced to express his views in an extremely subtle code—so subtle, in fact, that virtually all readers and critics have missed it until now.

Only in *Hamlet* does Shakespeare seem to show some awareness of the great issues of the Reformation, and even there he seems not to take sides. Asquith argues powerfully that, read carefully in its historical context, the play takes the Catholic side. She says the same is true of nearly all Shakespeare's plays, even those set in ancient Rome, pagan Britain, or on desert islands. To understand them we must "crack the code" that Shakespeare was forced to use in order to escape censorship.

How does this idea apply to *A Midsummer Night's Dream?* Here, if anywhere, is a play that seems to have nothing to do with the issues that divided Catholics and Protestants in the sixteenth century—a light comedy of lovers, fairies, and silly yokels set in a forest outside pre-Christian Athens. Nobody in the play says anything that is likely to remind us of the religious broils of Shakespeare's England many centuries later and thousands of miles away.

Of course this play, and all the others, may still be read in the traditional way, without any reference to the great wars of faith that divided the Christian world. But Asquith insists that if we read them that way, we are losing an essential dimension of their full meaning, because Shakespeare was a committed, secret, and illegal Catholic. He had to avoid persecution by writing his plays in a code that seemed to have nothing to do with religion, but which alert and sensitive Catholics in the audience might understand.

What was this code? According to Asquith, the moon symbolized Queen Elizabeth and the new religion brought by her father, Henry VIII. For example, the opening lines of *A Midsummer Night's Dream*, spoken by Theseus, complain "how slow this old moon wanes." This statement would

Scholar Clare Asquith believes that even Shakespeare's silliest plays have deeper religious meaning.

tip off Catholic spectators that the real subject was the old queen of England, whom, Catholics felt, had ruled the country for far too long.

Catholicism was symbolized by anything tall and fair, and Protestantism by the short and dark. The tall, fair Helena is symbolically Catholic, while Hermia, short and dark, is Protestant. The confusions of the four lovers become an allegory of England's religious strife, which Shakespeare hopes will end in reconciliation, just as the play ends in harmony.

Shakespeare himself, Asquith argues, appears as Bottom, hoping to please his rulers by entertaining them with a play. His very real fear of persecution is expressed comically in Bottom's seemingly absurd fear that he and his fellow actors may be "hanged" if they frighten the ladies in the audience.

In other plays, Asquith contends, an old order represents the Catholic England destroyed by Henry VIII and, currently, by his daughter Elizabeth. Even the plays set in ancient Rome before Julius Caesar overthrew the old republic and replaced it with an empire were meant to stand for the older, Catholic England. Likewise all usurpers, such as Macbeth, or Claudius in *Hamlet*, are meant to remind Shakespeare's Catholic audience of the Tudor tyranny that was sill trying to stamp out the popular old religion of Catholicism in England.

According to Asquith, Shakespeare was playing a very dangerous game. Under the seemingly nonreligious surface of his plays, he was taking the side of that older religion and its traditions against the new regime of the Tudor dynasty. Most scholars have seen Shakespeare's attitude as vaguely conservative, but until now nobody has thought of him as such a passionate partisan of the old, pre-Tudor social and religious order. If she is right, Asquith has given us a completely new conception of Shakespeare and a new key to interpreting his work, which nobody else has mentioned until now.

The Social Order in the Elizabethan World

Clare Asquith's argument about the role of religion in *A Midsummer Night's Dream* is not the only interpretation of the play that relies upon the context of the time in which the play was written. In his essay "A Kingdom of Shadows," Louis A. Montrose argues that the relationships and interplay among the characters in the play reflect and comment on the social order and world of Elizabethan England.

Part of Montrose's argument is the idea that the relationship between the spell-induced Titania and Bottom, as well as Bottom's relationship with the Duke, represent the multiple roles someone in Bottom's position would have had to inhabit. In one, he is temporarily elevated to the status of gentry but reminded by Titania that he must remain passive, a role that would've been prescribed for servants, children, and women; in the other role with the Duke, he is in a position of inferiority that borders on a childlike relationship to his social superior. The tradesmen in the play are in a similar position as they hope to better their social position through the patronage of the Duke. All of these roles would've found real-world counterparts in Elizabethan England.

Montrose goes on to argue that Bottom and the tradesmen in the play represent a certain class of artisans of the time; in fact, Montrose argues that Bottom in particular, by his name, represents a lowly position in the social order. The fact that he is named as a weaver may also speak to the food riots and social protests that took place during the mid-1590s, and weavers were especially associated with these riots. The character of Bottom also makes specific reference to the acting traditions of the times, traditions that Shakespeare obviously knew. Thus, Bottom gives voice not only to the dispossessed but to the professional players and playwrights of the time.

The time period in which Shakespeare was writing also included a decline in popular civic play forms. The title itself makes a nod toward some of these play forms, like the festival of Midsummer Eve that mixed together Christian and pagan traditions. These play forms are further referenced in Shakespeare's *Midsummer* by the naming of each of the tradesmen with their specific craft (i.e., Robin Starveling, the tailor; Nick Bottom, the weaver; Francis Flute, the bellows-mender; Tom Snout, the tinker; Snug the joiner).

As the tradesmen pull together to put on a play, it is important to note that they are doing so to entertain the ruler. According to Montrose, the play then has elements of courtly drama, suggesting that the playwright was ever aware of his royal audience (again, it is speculated that the play was written for a wedding that Queen Elizabeth attended). Yet what is significant is that there is no obvious representation of Queen Elizabeth in the play, and in the title page of the first quarto of *A Midsummer Night's Dream*, we see reference to the play having been performed publicly multiple times. In other words, despite the fact that Shakespeare and the Lord Chamberlain's Men were

A Midsummer Eve festival

supposed to be always in readiness for performance at court, it seems apparent that Shakespeare's plays were written with the possibility in mind of theatrical performance. This is important in that it speaks to the fact that the writing of plays included not only keeping in mind the audience of the court but also the audience of the common people; Shakespeare must have known that he was writing for both.

In writing for both, Shakespeare was situated at a significant and unique moment in history. He may have been speaking about the social and political order of his time, giving voice to the disenfranchised as well as to artists, along with not alienating the ruling class; he was also creating content and a form (the play within the play) that could expand beyond one particular age and find a place in countless social and political worlds.

CHRONOLOGY

1564 William Shakespeare is born on April 23 in Stratford-upon-Avon, England

1578–1582 Span of Shakespeare's "Lost Years," covering the time between leaving school and marrying Anne Hathaway of Stratford

1582 At age eighteen Shakespeare marries Anne Hathaway, age twenty-six, on November 28

1583 Susanna Shakespeare, William and Anne's first child, is born in May, six months after the wedding

1584 Birth of twins Hamnet and Judith Shakespeare

1585–1592 Shakespeare leaves his family in Stratford to become an actor and playwright in a London theater company

1587 Public beheading of Mary Queen of Scots

1593–94 The Bubonic (Black) Plague closes theaters in London

1594–96 As a leading playwright, Shakespeare creates some of his most popular work, including *A Midsummer Night's Dream* and *Romeo and Juliet*

1596 Hamnet Shakespeare dies in August at age eleven, possibly of plague

1596–97 *The Merchant of Venice* and *Henry IV, Part One* most likely are written

1599 The Globe Theatre opens

1600 *Julius Caesar* is first performed at the Globe

1600–01 *Hamlet* is believed to have been written

1601–02 *Twelfth Night* is probably composed

1603 Queen Elizabeth dies; Scottish king James VI succeeds her and becomes England's James I

1604 Shakespeare pens *Othello*

1605 *Macbeth* is composed

1608–1610 London's theaters are forced to close when the plague returns and kills an estimated 33,000 people

1611 *The Tempest* is written

1613 The Globe Theatre is destroyed by fire

1614 Reopening of the Globe

1616 Shakespeare dies on April 23

1623 Anne Hathaway, Shakespeare's widow, dies; a collection of Shakespeare's plays, known as the First Folio, is published

A SHAKESPEARE GLOSSARY

addition A name or title, such as knight, duke, duchess, king, etc.

affect To like or love; to be attracted to.

approve To prove or confirm.

attend To pay attention.

belike Probably.

beseech To beg or request.

bondman A slave.

bootless Futile; useless; in vain.

broil A battle.

charge Expense, responsibility; to command or accuse.

common A term describing the common people, below nobility.

condition Social rank; quality.

countenance Face; appearance; favor.

cousin A relative.

curious Careful; attentive to detail.

discourse To converse; conversation.

discover To reveal or uncover.

dispatch To speed or hurry; to send; to kill.

doubt To suspect.

entreat To beg or appeal.

envy To hate or resent; hatred; resentment.

ere Before.

eyne Eyes.

fain Gladly.

fare To eat; to prosper.

favor Face, privilege.

fellow A peer or equal.

filial Of a child toward its parent.

fine An end; "in fine" means in sum.

folio A book made up of individually printed sheets, each folded in half to make four pages; Shakespeare's folios contain all of his known plays in addition to other works.

fond Foolish.

fool A darling.

genius A good or evil spirit.

gentle Well-bred; not common.

gentleman One whose labor was done by servants. (Note: to call someone a gentleman was not a mere compliment on his manners; it meant that he was above the common people.)

gentles People of quality.

get To beget (a child).

go to "Go on"; "come off it."

go we Let us go.

haply Perhaps.

happily By chance; fortunately.

hard by Nearby.

heavy Sad or serious.

husbandry Thrift; economy.

instant Immediate.

kind One's nature; species.

knave A villain; a poor man.

lady A woman of high social rank. (Note: lady was not a synonym for woman or polite woman; it was not a compliment but simply a word referring to one's actual legal status in society, like gentleman.)

leave Permission; "take my leave" means depart (with permission).

lief, lieve "I had as lief " means I would just as soon; I would rather.

like To please; "it likes me not" means it is disagreeable to me.

livery The uniform of a nobleman's servants; emblem.

Lord Chamberlain's Men The company of players Shakespeare joined in London; under James I they became the King's Men.

mark Notice; pay attention.

morrow Morning.

needs Necessarily.

nice Too fussy or fastidious.

owe To own.

passing Very.

peculiar Individual; exclusive.

privy Private; secret.

proper Handsome; one's very own ("his proper son").

protest To insist or declare.

quite Completely.

require Request.

several Different, various.

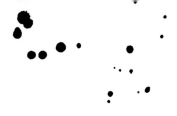

severally Separately.

sirrah A term used to address social inferiors.

sooth Truth.

state Condition; social rank.

still Always; persistently.

success Result(s).

surfeit Fullness.

touching Concerning; about; as for.

translate To transform.

understatement A statement expressing less than intended, often with an ironic or comic intention; the opposite of hyperbole.

unfold To disclose.

verse Writing that uses a regular metrical rhythm and is divided from other lines by a space.

villain A low or evil person; originally, a peasant.

voice A vote; consent; approval.

vouchsafe To confide or grant.

vulgar Common.

want To lack.

weeds Clothing.

what ho "Hello, there!"

wherefore Why.

wit Intelligence; sanity.

withal Moreover; nevertheless.

without Outside.

would Wish.

SUGGESTED ESSAY TOPICS

1. Do you think any of the characters of *A Midsummer Night's Dream* speak for Shakespeare? Why or why not?

2. What does Theseus tell us, and illustrate, about the nature of a wise ruler?

3. How does Bottom, a mere weaver, "steal" the play from the other, seemingly more important characters?

4. Pagan gods such as Venus, Cupid, Phoebe, and Neptune are often mentioned but never actually appear in the play. How do they influence the events of the story?

TEST YOUR MEMORY

1. Puck replaces Bottom's head with that of a) A dog.
b) A lion. c) An ass. d) A bear.

2. Bottom and his friends act out the story of a) Romeo
and Juliet. b) Pyramus and Thisby. c) Antony and
Cleopatra. d) Adam and Eve.

3. Theseus is a) King of the forest. b) Duke of Athens.
c) Emperor of Rome. d) A Greek god.

4. Hippolyta is a) Queen of the Amazons. b) Princess of
Egypt. c) Duchess of York. d) A rich widow.

5. Oberon is a) A carpenter. b) King of the fairies.
c) An elf. d) A hunter.

6. After his transformation, Bottom feels a sudden craving
for a) Hay. b) Wine. c) Beef. d) Salt water.

7. When Lysander is under Puck's spell, he a) Thinks he
is mad. b) Runs away from Athens. c) Decides to find
Bottom. d) Falls in love with Helena.

8. Puck is also known as a) Robin Goodfellow. b) Cupid.
c) A mermaid. d) Peter Quince.

9. Egeus asks Theseus to a) Delay his wedding to
Hippolyta. b) Force Hermia to marry Demetrius.
c) Kill Lysander. d) Cancel the play.

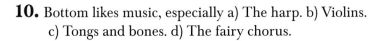

10. Bottom likes music, especially a) The harp. b) Violins.
c) Tongs and bones. d) The fairy chorus.

11. When the play is performed, one of the actors plays
a) Hamlet. b) The king. c) A fairy. d) Moonshine.

12. Oberon and Titania quarrel over a) A little boy.
b) Bottom. c) Puck. d) Thisby.

13. Bottom calls the play he stars in a) A tragedy.
b) A comedy. c) A satire. d) A musical.

14. The actors are afraid of a) Making Theseus angry.
b) Not being funny. c) Frightening the ladies. d) The lion.

15. Back to normal, Bottom thinks he has a) Seen ghosts.
b) Met Puck. c) Become a great actor. d) Had a
beautiful dream.

16. After learning of the planned elopement, Helena decides
to a) Tell Demetrius. b) Steal Lysander from Hermia.
c) Seek the fairies. d) Play a prank on Bottom's friends.

17. According to Helena, Cupid is said to be a) Cruel.
b) Musical. c) Untrustworthy. d) Blind.

18. Titania thinks Bottom is a) In disguise.
b) Wise and beautiful. c) Ignorant. d) A fairy.

19. Oberon tells Puck that he has actually seen a) Cupid. b) Theseus. c) Bottom. d) A sea monster.

20. Hippolyta thinks Bottom's play is a) Deeply moving. b) Silly. c) Too long. d) Obscene.

Answer Key

1.c; 2. b; 3. b; 4. a; 5. b; 6. a; 7. d; 8. a; 9. b; 10. c; 11. d; 12. a; 13. a; 14. c; 15. d; 16. a; 17. d; 18. b; 19. a; 20. b

FURTHER INFORMATION

Books

Bates, Laura. *Shakespeare Saved My Life: Ten Years in Solitary with the Bard.* Naperville, IL: Sourcebooks, 2013.

Bryson, Bill. *Shakespeare: The World As Stage.* New York: Harper Collins, 2007.

Cambridge School Shakespeare. *A Midsummer Night's Dream.* Cambridge: Cambridge University Press, 2014.

McDonald, John. *A Midsummer Night's Dream: The Graphic Novel.* Lichtborough: Classical Comics, 2011.

Websites

Folger Shakespeare Library
http://www.folger.edu

The Folger Shakespeare Library is home to the world's largest Shakespeare collection, and this online resource for the library contains digital versions of the plays as well as vast amounts of research on the plays and life of Shakespeare.

Royal Shakespeare Company

http://www.rsc.org.uk

This website provides information about the Royal Shakespeare Company and its history and current theater productions of Shakespeare's works in his hometown of Stratford-upon-Avon as well as information about Shakespeare's life and plays.

Shakespeare's Words

http://www.shakespeareswords.com

This online companion to the book *Shakespeare's Words: A Glossary and Language Companion* contains digital versions of the plays and poems as well as a searchable glossary for better understanding Shakespeare's language while reading his works.

Films

A Midsummer Night's Dream, directed by Peter Hall; with David Warner, Diana Rigg, Judi Dench, and Helen Mirren, 1968.

A Midsummer Night's Dream, directed by Michael Hoffman; with Kevin Kline, Michelle Pfeiffer, and Stanley Tucci, 1999.

A Midsummer Night's Dream: Shakespeare's Globe Theatre On-Screen, directed by Dominic Dromgoole, 2015.

BIBLIOGRAPHY

"Bard on the Beach Shakespeare Festival." *Bardonthebeach.org.* Accessed April 28, 2016. http://bardonthebeach.org.

Bate, Jonathan, and Eric Rasmussen, eds. *William Shakespeare Complete Works (Modern Library).* New York: Random House, 2007.

Bloom, Harold. *Shakespeare: The Invention of the Human.* New York: Riverhead Books, Burgess, Anthony. *Shakespeare.* New York: Alfred A. Knopf, 1970.

Calderwood, James L. *Twayne's New Critical Introductions to Shakespeare: A Midsummer Night's Dream.* New York: Twayne, 1992.

Chute, Marchette. *Shakespeare of London.* New York: Dutton, 1949.

Clark, Sandra. *NTC's Dictionary of Shakespeare: A Comprehensive Guide to Shakespeare's Plays, Characters, and Contemporaries.* Lincolnwood, IL: NTC Publishing Group, 1997.

"The Dell." *Royal Shakespeare Company.org.* Accessed April 28, 2016. https://www.rsc.org.uk/events/the-dell.

"Free Shakespeare in the Park." *Public Theater.org.* Accessed May 2, 2016. http://www.publictheater.org/en/Free-Shakespeare-in-the-Park/.

Garber, Marjorie. *Shakespeare After All.* New York: Pantheon, 2004.

——. *Shakespeare and Modern Culture.* New York: Pantheon, 2008.

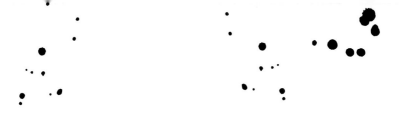

Goddard, Harold C. *The Meaning of Shakespeare*. Chicago: University of Chicago Press, 1951.

Greenblatt, Stephen. *Will in the World: How Shakespeare Became Shakespeare*. New York: W. W. Norton & Company, 2004.

Hirsh, James. Shakespeare and the History of Soliloquies. London: Fairleigh Dickinson University Press, 2003. PDF e-book.

Honan, Park. *Shakespeare: A Life*. New York: Oxford University Press, 1998.

McElroy, Steven. "What Creators These Mortals Be." *New York Times*, June 13, 2013. http://www.nytimes. com/2013/06/16/theater/a-midsummer-nights-dream-in-different-looks-and-cities.html?_r=1.

Montrose, Louis A. "A Kingdom of Shadows." *In A Midsummer Night's Dream: Critical Essays*, Edited by Dorothea Kehler. New York: Garland Publishing, 1998.

"Popular Songs Inspired By Shakespeare." *CBC Music*. Last modified April 14, 2014. Accessed May 6, 2016. http://music.cbc.ca/#!/blogs/2014/4/Popular-songs-inspired-by-Shakespeare.

"Public Works." *Public Theater.org*. Accessed May 2, 2016. http://www.publictheater.org/en/Programs–Events/Public-Works/

Rafael, Burton. ed. *A Midsummer Night's Dream: The Annotated Shakespeare*. New Haven, CT: Yale University Press, 2005.

Schoenbaum, Samuel. *William Shakespeare: A Documentary Life.* New York: Oxford University Press, 1975.

——. *William Shakespeare: Records and Images.* New York: Oxford University Press, 1981.

Traversi, D. L. *An Approach to Shakespeare.* Palo Alto, CA: Stanford University Press, 1957.

Van Doren, Mark. *Shakespeare.* Garden City, NY: Doubleday, 1939.

INDEX

ABOUT THE AUTHORS

Patricia Wagner is an educator who works primarily with high school students. She enjoys writing about the intersection of history and literature. Wagner is currently researching Thomas Kyd, one of Shakespeare's contemporaries. In her free time, Wagner paints and spends time with her seven grandchildren. She recently relocated to the West Coast to be closer to them, and she enjoys visiting Lake Tahoe whenever possible.

Summar West is a writer and poet whose works have been published in a variety of literary journals, including *491 Magazine, Appalachian Heritage, Appalachian Journal, Ellipsis, Numero Cinq, Still: the Journal, Tar River Poetry,* and more. She is a professor of writing and literature and enjoys teaching in a variety of classroom and non-traditional settings. She first fell in love with the language of Shakespeare in her freshman English class in high school and has been reading, researching, and interpreting the Bard's works since then. Beyond her love of books and art, her interests also include running, hiking, biking, and other activities that allow her to be outdoors.